The Expert Guide to Retail Pricing

T0293127

Going under the hood of retail strategy, this book provides in-depth coverage of how retailers can leverage the latest in data analytics and technology to improve profitability and customer value through pricing. Retail pricing is not about dollars, pounds, or euros, but the value a customer associates with a product, which can and does change over time. To maximise revenues and profits, pricing must be dynamic, strategic, and in today's hyper-connected and competitive world, scientific. Using technology to gather customer insights and create data-driven pricing approaches can also enhance the customer experience, improve vendor management, help monitor competitors, and ensure market efficiency – including the much-needed reduction of waste in the food sector. This book uses case studies from around the globe to illustrate the evolution of retailing and offers takeaways with each chapter to enable retailers to manage the future of pricing. Retail and pricing managers, retail sector consultants, and students of sales and marketing will welcome this book's innovative solutions to one of bricks-and-mortar retailing's most critical challenges.

Kiran Gange
CEO/ Founder at RapidPricer B.V.
linkedin.com/in/kirangange
kirangange@gmail.com
www.kirangange.com

Kiran Gange is the CEO and founder of RapidPricer, an Artificial Intelligence based company in Amsterdam that specialises in reducing food waste through real-time pricing for retailers. Previously, he founded CustoLogix in the year 2008 to help retailers leverage analytics and mathematical capabilities for pricing and promotions. Recently, Kiran also founded Global Launch Base, an internationalisation consulting firm in 2021 which helps European companies with international go-to-market strategies and market launches. He has over 16 years of experience launching innovative technologies around the world. He has consulted on behalf of large consulting companies such as PwC, IBM, and Kurt Salmon at some of the largest retailers in the world. His entrepreneurial experiences include successful ventures in Silicon Valley, Mexico City, Bangalore, Amsterdam, and New Delhi. He holds a bachelor's degree in mechanical engineering with honors from the Bangalore Institute of Technology and an MBA from Pepperdine University on a full-merit scholarship. Kiran is a powerful speaker and a writer with the ability to motivate and lead teams to pursue vision towards impactful goals. He has the ability to connect with multicultural teams and has trained startup founders on entrepreneurship and retail technologies at several prestigious institutions and organisations such as the U.C. Berkeley in California and the Professional Pricing Society in Atlanta, US. In his spare time, Kiran enjoys photography and works with young entrepreneurs.

The Expert Guide to Retail Pricing

An Analytics-Based Approach to Maximise Margins

Kiran Gange

Routledge
Taylor & Francis Group

NEW YORK AND LONDON

Designed cover image: Getty

First published 2024
by Routledge
605 Third Avenue, New York, NY 10158

and by Routledge
4 Park Square, Milton Park, Abingdon, Oxon, OX14 4RN

Routledge is an imprint of the Taylor & Francis Group, an informa business

Library of Congress Cataloguing-in-Publication Data
Names: Gange, Kiran, author.
Title: The expert guide to retail pricing : an analytics-based approach to maximise margins / Kiran Gange.
Description: New York, NY : Routledge, 2023. | Includes bibliographical references and index. |
Identifiers: LCCN 2023003229 (print) | LCCN 2023003230 (ebook) | ISBN 9781032465333 (hardback) | ISBN 9781032465326 (paperback) | ISBN 9781003382140 (ebook)
Subjects: LCSH: Pricing. | Retail trade.
Classification: LCC HF5416.5 .G36 2023 (print) | LCC HF5416.5 (ebook) | DDC 658.8/16--dc23/eng/20230125
LC record available at https://lccn.loc.gov/2023003229
LC ebook record available at https://lccn.loc.gov/2023003230

ISBN: 978-1-032-46533-3 (hbk)
ISBN: 978-1-032-46532-6 (pbk)
ISBN: 978-1-003-38214-0 (ebk)

DOI: 10.4324/9781003382140

Typeset in Bembo
by MPS Limited, Dehradun

Contents

Foreword   *vi*
Preface   *ix*
Acknowledgements   *xi*

Introduction   1

1   Impact of Pricing   6

2   Base Pricing   33

3   Promotions   73

4   Markdown   95

5   Competitive Pricing   112

6   Business Intelligence   129

7   E-Commerce Pricing   145

8   Future of Pricing   170

Conclusion   184

Index   *187*

Foreword

When I was given the opportunity to write the foreword for this book, I jumped at the chance. After spending almost 20 years helping companies with pricing, the value of a clear, comprehensive guide for retailers was obvious to me. While there are a number of books available on retail pricing theory, there is a real need for one that takes that theory and supplements it with pricing approaches, tactics, technologies, and processes. This is that book, and this is what allows merchants to truly drive financial impact through pricing. There are really three things that stood out to me about this guide. The first is subject. Pricing is an often underappreciated part of retailing and any book that helps drive investment into this critical area is of great value. The second is how complex and dynamic pricing has become. This book, with its inclusion of topics like price optimisation, electronic shelf labels, and real-time algorithms could not have been written when I first started working with retailers. The third is the breadth of knowledge that Kiran Gange brings as an author. His decades of real-world experience drive a concise and useful narrative.

My kids can't believe I find pricing so interesting. I try to explain to them how important it is for a business. I expect many readers already fully understand the impact pricing can have on a retailer's bottom line. But it helps to reiterate that pricing is the strongest lever for profitability that a retailer has. US grocery chains have averaged a net profit of just 2% over the last 20 years (per the Food Industry Association). This means if you could raise prices by just 1% without losing volume (theoretically) it would translate to a massive increase in net profits. This leverage is incredible. On the flip side, if you increase prices too much, and you damage your price reputation, volume can drop, you can't support your fixed costs, and you are quickly in a world of pain. There are dozens of former retail chains that went from success to bankruptcy when a rival was perceived as consistently offering a better deal. You can ask anyone who competed with Walmart in the early 2000s how true this is.

The importance of pricing is so great that it is the prime criteria Warren Buffet uses to determine whether or not to invest in a business. In an interview, Buffet said "The single-most important decision in evaluating a business is pricing power. If you've got the power to raise prices without losing business to a competitor, you've got a very good business. And if you have to have a prayer session before raising the price by a tenth of a cent, then you've got a terrible business. I've been in both, and I know the difference". It is this importance that makes books like this so valuable. Pricing acumen can literally be the difference between long-term success and failure for a retailer.

Besides the value of pricing, people need to know more about pricing technologies and capabilities. This book clearly shows how pricing has undergone as dramatic a shift in the last 25 years as any process in any company. Twenty-five years ago, most retail chains priced with simple margin or markup rules and had a basket of goods they might cross-shop against competitors. This wasn't even basic rules-based pricing, because the lack of systems didn't allow the consistent enforcement of simple logic – like a larger size product should be a better unit value than a smaller product. However, since all retailers were like this, simplistic error-prone pricing was accepted. Today there are many retailers who are using machine learning and artificial intelligence to determine the best price for a specific product at a specific point in time in a specific location. Online retailers often have dynamic pricing where algorithms determine the price based on real-time competitive intelligence, and inventory levels, and adjust for individual customers.

This shift in technology, approach, data, and process is amazing by itself but it happened in an environment where SKUs proliferation has exploded, supply chains have become more complex, and customers have been given their own set of tools to rapidly cross-check prices. All in all, pricing is radically different from what it used to be and this book outlines pricing practices and technologies from the simple to the most sophisticated.

If anyone was to write a book that distilled key information about pricing in the face of all the recent changes it makes sense then it is Kiran. I started working with Kiran Gange about 20 years ago and have followed his career closely ever since. I think he is in a unique position to write this book. Many previous books on pricing have been written by academics who write theory and others by management consultants who debate strategy. Very few have been written by someone who built and implemented systems for many different retailers to specifically improve pricing and were accountable for measurable margin improvement. In Kiran's career, he didn't drop off pricing strategy recommendations and walk away. Instead, Kiran has helped retailers turn their strategy into price tags and those price tags into dollars. Kiran has been responsible for taking general margin goals, defining a strategy, and translating that down through robust systems and processes to set the best price for a pair of headphones going into the Christmas season in a store in Dallas, or spinach that is a day away from expiring at a grocer in Paris, or this week's key promotional item at an online fashion retailer. His experience is hands-on and broad-based and it has included small retailers and the world's largest chains. He has worked on pricing throughout a product's lifecycle and he has worked with retailers at all stages of pricing maturity.

In any case, whether you are a grizzled pricing veteran trying to see what other players are doing in the industry, a person new to pricing, a retail executive, a category manager with financial goals, or just someone who is interested in learning how new technologies and approaches are transforming a critical business function I think you will benefit from this book.

John O'Connor

https://www.linkedin.com/in/john-o-connor-09a196/

Preface

I started working in retail when I was 12 years old when I started working in a retail store that was less than 150 Sq.ft in size. My parents had decided that my summer holidays could be put to good use by learning how businesses worked in real life.

Later on, I became an engineer, more to please society than for my passion. I was much rather enjoying organising events and playing soccer, and I couldn't wait to pack my mathematics and technical books up the attic so I could get into business. In a few years, I had an MBA from the beautiful Pepperdine University in California. Here you were allowed to have open books for exams which was a strange but interesting concept for me. Our finals, for example, were being judged by how useful the local surf shop in Malibu thought my business plans for their retail store were.

My first real job was that of an analyst in the retail industry again. I travelled Monday to Thursday to some of the largest retail headquarters in the United States. Two years into it, just as I really enjoyed the consulting aspect of the retail strategy, I interviewed with the CEO of a very successful retail firm called Fry's Electronics. The CEO, John Fry asked me to come work for him directly. He was also the president of the American Institute of Mathematics and had grand ideas for building new algorithms for retail challenges. Back came my Mathematical books, John Fry did not want to implement anything I did not understand to the core. At the same time, he said he didn't care about where I got the work done as long as I got the results. Thus started my first start-up. A team of analysts and mathematicians supported me in my full-time job to reduce inventories and plan retail promotions for Fry's Electronics. I also went back to my first consulting job and told them I would still do my job for half the money. They liked the offer.

By 2011, I had quit my full-time job while still supporting Fry's Electronics, my old consulting employer and many more clients I had acquired along the way. By 2017, I had implemented enough pricing implementations around the world to realise that the challenges faced, the journeys undertaken, and the results being achieved through a science-based pricing approach were very similar.

This is when I started my second company RapidPricer to automate pricing by standardising the usual processes. This book is about these standardised best practices that have always delivered increased margins and successes for retailers.

In my journey, I have also briefly opened my own convenience store and sat at the checkout counter on many nights and weekends to connect mathematical algorithms to the real business world. I hope this book will be of use to retailers, retail professionals, and students interested in the world of retail and retail pricing.

The contents described in the book are what I personally term "traditional science-based pricing". While this should be the first step most retailers should adopt to improve their pricing function, the future of retail pricing belongs to price automation. I am currently fully immersed in the goal of retail price automation with RapidPricer in Amsterdam and working to reduce food waste in retail as a result of this dynamic and automated pricing based on artificial intelligence.

My vision is to create a world where people gain more value and create less waste from every product purchased through innovation and technology.

Acknowledgements

I would like to thank the wonderful team I have supporting me through my other start-up Global Launch Base. Special thanks to Anubha Chicki for being supportive, hiring, and managing an all-girls team of talented team members. Seetarama Hegde remains one of the first and most valuable team members in all our pricing projects.

Gargi Sarma has worked tirelessly to support me with various research and to prepare the analysis that was required to support this book. Mamta Devi has been a real gem helping the team with all the design requirements. Thanks also to Jagriti Shahi for supporting the analysis needed for the key chapters in the book.

I would like to add special thanks to my mentors in Retail who have taught me much about how both science and artwork in retail. This includes John Fry, John O'Connor, Sean Kervin, Lance Golinghorst, Nuri Mehmet, and John Chao.

Last but not least, I would like to thank my business partners and shareholders who have trusted and supported me immensely in many phases of my retail pricing journey. This includes Lohith Amrendra, Ellen Bark-Lindhout, Mike Rogers, Harm Nijlunsing, and Jan-Willem Jonker.

Kiran Gange

Introduction

Retail Pricing is one of the most critical functions within a retail business. Not only is price a key determining factor in purchasing a product, but it also plays a vital role in many other aspects of the retail business such as price image, market share, and customer loyalty.

Pricing in retail can be defined as the value put on a product or service at the point of purchase. This value is not constant. It fluctuates constantly. It is different for different consumers at different points in time. However, the price at which a retailer sells can be constant for months together – this inherent mismatch of price and value results in market inefficiencies. The result is either the consumer paying a price less than the value the person places on the product or the consumer not being able to afford the price as it is beyond the value the person places on the product.

The value placed by each customer on a product depends on the need for the product at the time of purchase. This also depends on the prices of the substitutable set of products and the price for the same product in the market. Perhaps, even the weather, day of the week, time of the day, and, in some cases, a customer's salary date.

Having the right price for each purchase may enable consumers to buy a larger number of affordable products. The retailer may benefit by selling more products, reducing wastage, and making more profit which can enable more business growth and employment opportunities. However, the right price is different for each consumer, perhaps different at different times of the day. Is this even possible? Well, yes, some online retail giants already change their prices based on customer demographics, time, and other user behaviour on a continuous basis. This differentiation has made them hugely successful and profitable that too by having happy consumers. According to a recent report, Amazon changed the price of each product on average every 10 minutes.

This book is about how retailers can master the art of this win-win pricing that will ensure market efficiency: where consumers can afford more products and high profit for retailers.

In the following chapters, we will discuss the various pillars of retail strategy that form the backbone for an efficient pricing process for retail stores. Scientific

DOI: 10.4324/9781003382140-1

pricing allows retailers to enhance a customer's experience, whether in-store or online, by using best practices in strategy, economics, and mathematics to achieve the desired market efficiency. This book outlines the benefits and limitations of scientific retail pricing. It includes case studies of retailers from various industries who have effectively used these tools and approaches.

This book also deals with recent developments in retail pricing optimisation and evolving pricing practices. We start by looking at how retailers usually make pricing selections based on time-tested observations to determine the best options.

However, traditional approaches can be inefficient because they ignore the effects of demand on the pricing of the product and are usually based on the cost of the product. The traditional pricing approaches also tend to ignore the dynamic impact of seasonality, competition, weather, and other factors. Most traditional pricing approaches do not consider how price elasticity changes over time; for example, in items with short shelf lives, such as fresh produce, or how different market segments react to price increases differently.

Many retailers also struggle to determine how to price items when their suppliers offer limited-time specials and are often unaware of the impact their pricing approach has on their overall image. Optimal pricing is not a static problem. Changes in the environment or sales patterns require retailers to react swiftly. This book includes examples of advanced pricing approaches that are now being tried in the real world. Finally, we will go through the key elements that must be considered for developing a pricing system for retail organisations.

Market dynamics are reasonably predictable in normal times. However, the Covid-19 pandemic the world witnessed was not a "normal" time. Retailers in several countries had to close down outlets. E-commerce almost overnight became a viable alternative and, in some circumstances, the only option for purchasing items. Engagement with e-commerce hit an all-time high in countries that were unfamiliar with online purchasing. Electronic payment systems also improved efficiency and security, offering customers a dependable solution for payments. To attract customers, retailers expanded their product lines and looked into a variety of sales channels and pricing methods.

Although brick-and-mortar sales of retail are now back to their original levels, the pandemic not only pushed e-commerce to previously unheard-of levels but also the emergence of new business intelligence strategies and algorithms.

Most traditional pricing approaches are based on costs. While this approach is easy and safe, it is a very inefficient way to price a product. The driver behind the price for every product should be the customer's demand for the product. In almost all cases, the cost of manufacturing a product does not have any connection to the customer's demand. Hence the retailer who chooses a cost-plus-based pricing strategy is inherently operating at inefficient prices, which results in the prices being too high for customers or too low to accommodate a sufficient profit for the retailer.

While science-based price optimisation, perhaps even in real-time, might be an ideal goal, oftentimes, retailers might need to take several intermediary strategies to move away from cost-based pricing strategies.

Below is a brief introduction to various pricing strategies for increasing levels of efficiency and profitability.

1   Rules-Based Pricing: One of the most important techniques and easy fixes to do in retail pricing is called Rules-Based Pricing. A simple walk through a store shelf oftentimes can reveal many glaring mistakes in pricing, which can be both confusing for the consumer and loss-making for a retailer. Retailers can set a wide variety and simple rules to make sure all the prices in all stores comply with these rules. These rules can be simple rules such as line pricing, size rules, competitive rules, margin rules, last digit ending rules, and even category role-based rules. Oftentimes, this can be accomplished in a simple spreadsheet with algebraic formulas.

2   Market-Based Pricing: Once we have a good understanding of the basic pricing rules, a retailer should look at their own environment to make sure their pricing strategy is in line with the needs of the market. Frequently retailers operate in highly competitive and evolved marketplaces, which means the other competitors in the market can hold several valuable lessons that can help the retailer establish their own pricing strategies. A simple comparison of prices of the top-selling items to nearby competitors can reveal many opportunities in pricing. For example, a competitor might be selling milk or eggs at prices significantly lower and leading traffic away. On the other hand, there might be a high-priced holiday gift that is being sold at a much higher price in the market place which could allow a retailer to increase his own price. While competitive pricing can become much more data-driven and scientific, a good place to start is a simple process to note and track the prices of a retailer's competition.

3   Science-Based Pricing: Using data to complement intuition can be a powerful combination. The core material of this book is dedicated to helping retailers understand and device data and science-based processes for retail pricing. This will include strategy formulation, category and product role definitions, pricing rules, competitive strategy, price optimisation, and price maintenance.

4   Real-Time Pricing: Once a robust framework for data management and pricing is set in place. It can be the right time to move tasks towards automation. Several tasks, such as reacting to cost changes, competitive price changes, and even change in the product's value (such as a banana changing from green to yellow), can be connected to automatic price changes. This, however, requires certain hardware components such as Electronic Shelf Labels and various in-store sensing technologies.

5   Customer Level Pricing: As retailing continues to evolve towards becoming more of a commodity, customers will demand a higher level of customisation

for their own individual needs. As is already evident in some segments of retail. The future of retail will mean the demands of the consumers will be met with as little friction as possible at the right price and at the right time, which will be unique for each customer. For example, imagine a situation where a sensor enables a fitness t-shirt to work with an algorithm to replenish the right nutrients for the wearer into his kitchen with an order timed to arrive in time at the right price automatically.

A retailer should critically examine where it stands in the retail evolution cycle in its own marketplace. The goal towards higher efficiency in retail is a continuous journey that should never end. However, it is always a good idea to utilise the best practices that have already evolved through innovations and experiments across the globe.

Traditional retailers have resistance to changing their pricing strategy, it is rightly identified as one of the most important factors in the profitability and survival of the business. In the past, retailers have relied on intuition and standardised safe processes such as cost-based pricing. Still, the need to adopt a more efficient process is critical in today's competitive environment.

Most retailers do not utilise price as a basis for creating a permanent competitive advantage since low-price strategies are too easy for competitors to adopt. Only a few retailers can succeed with a pure low-cost–low-price approach. Price can, however, always be utilised strategically, even if it is not always to determine the lowest price.

Until recently, retailers' initial pricing and subsequent markdown decisions to drop the price and value of a product to boost sales were often based on arbitrary principles that they believed had worked well in the past. Today, various specialised organisations have developed methodologies and tools to assist retailers in making these critical pricing decisions.

Many retailers today use price and promotion optimisation software. Controlled field tests show that their solution routinely beats the control group in improving profit while maintaining or increasing sales and market share depending on the retailer's desired goals. Furthermore, planning assortments, initial pricing, sourcing/vendor coordination, buying, item allocation to stores, promotion, planning replenishment, space management, and markdown pricing are just a few of the decision-making tools accessible to retailers.

While it is important to adapt retailing practices to the established best practices in scientific retailing, it should also be noted that retailers do not have to understand every component of pricing science to its core to leverage the science. For example, the most efficient ride from an airport to a conference might be by calling a cab through an app, there is simply no need to understand the mechanisms of a combustion engine or a carburettor. Similarly, retailers can use several tools and existing algorithms to establish a pricing strategy that is right for them instead of having to hire and train the world's best data scientists, data engineers, or hardware developers.

The upcoming chapters aim to investigate developing retail pricing practices and uncover pricing opportunities across time. This includes initial pricing, promotion, markdown pricing decisions, category/assortment management decisions, and other technology-enabled tools and processes that help retailers with profitable growth.

Chapter 1

Impact of Pricing

1.1 Introduction

In the previous chapter, we saw how Retail Pricing is one of the most important functions of a retail organisation. The price of a product determines the value the retailer places on the product to be sold. However, this value has little to do with the actual value a customer is willing to pay for the product. Especially if the same price is used across all markets and for all customer segments, there will be huge mismatches between the price of the product and the value a customer places on it in different stores and times. If the price marked for a product by the retailer is too high, the product will not be purchased by a customer, and it will remain unsold. For a purchase to happen, a product needs to be priced at or below the value of the product as perceived by the purchaser. This is true not only when a customer buys a product from a retailer but also holds true when a retailer purchases a product from a vendor. On the other hand, if the retailer marks a price that is too low for a consumer, then the retailer might lose profit opportunities using which he could address a larger market. Ideally, the retailer should reduce where a consumer demands a lower price and increase it where a consumer can afford a higher price.

To maximise the efficiency of a market, products should be priced at their "optimal" price when a market is considered to be performing at its peak efficiency. Consumers are able to buy more products that might otherwise go unsold – simultaneously, retailers are able to maximise profits and address a larger market. Note that the optimal prices can be lower or higher than the current price. Usually, retailers use a "cost-plus" or "margin-based" pricing strategy to sell products at a "fair" price. However, a buying customer has no regard for what the retailer actually paid for the product the customer wishes to buy. To reinstate, the major factor that determines a customer's decision to buy a product is simply the comparison between the customer's value for the product at that point in time and the associated price.

Any product can and will have different values for different customers. A product may also hold a different value for the same customer at different points in time. Also, a change in value or demand will occur for a product in different locations. For example, a cell phone charger that is sold at an airport has a very

DOI: 10.4324/9781003382140-2

different value when compared to the same charger being sold at a supermarket in a suburban location. Now, imagine if a retailer were to charge the same price at both locations. At the airport location, the retailer will end up losing money on each transaction due to the high cost of the rent. At the suburban supermarket, a customer will find the same charger unaffordable. Therefore, the right strategy here would be to raise the price at the airport and lower it at the suburban store.

Another example would be to offer a lower price for, say, essential food supplies in a low-income neighbourhood. However, raise the price for the same product in a high-income neighbourhood. Not only are the costs associated with carrying the products in each of these locations different, but the willingness to pay for these products is also different. Not having a differentiated pricing strategy by location, in this case, will result in more hungry people in a low-income neighbourhood and, perhaps, excess supplies in the rich neighbourhood resulting in lost profit for the retailer operating in each of the stores.

Many retailers often do and should set the prices differently in different locations. Often, the pricing zones are based on simplistic geographies and districts. It makes business sense to create these pricing zones based on the value buckets for the customers. Such as high-income versus low-income or urban versus suburban stores. For overall efficiency, it is better to price each product on the willingness to pay by the customer. Though this may not be easily possible within the confines of a brick-and-mortar store, retailers can easily do so for online customers. Retailers may also employ couponing for each individual brick-and-mortar customer. The airline industry, driven by the constant pressure to operate at maximum efficiency while selling a commodity or service, figured this out a long time ago. There is a need and opportunity for other industries, including retail, to follow this differentiation.

As time goes by, a product does not hold the same value on the retail shelf. Consider a new product launch, winter wear, air conditioners, or fresh produce. With time, the value a customer is willing to pay for each of these products on the retail shelf changes continuously. Now, if each product is not sold at the right price throughout its lifecycle, there could be product shortages at the beginning of the lifecycle and a pile-up of unsold inventory towards the end of the life cycle resulting in wastage and losses. It would be profitable to launch a new technology headphone at a higher price in the beginning and gradually ramp down its price before a new product that can replace it is launched.

Similarly, it would be a good strategy to drop the price of woollens towards the end of winter, as the customer is less willing to pay the same price. A good strategy, in this case, would be to start low at the beginning of the season, the highest price just before the peak of winter and thereafter drop the price based on inventory and weather conditions forecasted in each location to sell out the inventory with the end of the season. This will allow customers to buy a product at the value they would place on it, the retailers to make a high profit, and factories to produce more goods resulting in overall market efficiency.

Arriving at the optimal price requires the following chain of events: a good understanding of the markets, timely access to relevant market data, the ability to process this information, make the right decision, execute this decision on time at the store, measure the results, and improve the prices in real-time based on the changing conditions. It may seem like a daunting task to accomplish the goal of optimal pricing on a continuous basis. Still, many retailers utilise established best practices and technologies to achieve stellar profits and growth opportunities by leveraging science into every operation.

Based on the level of sophistication and technology deployed, retailers can begin their pricing journeys at different starting points. For example, a retailer can start with a simple analysis in a spreadsheet to achieve quick and significant wins are deploy sophisticated artificial intelligence-enabled automated pricing algorithms to bring down food wastage to near zero levels. Achieving a more mature pricing system will require investments in hardware, processes, and resources with a vision and conviction to achieve the desired results.

1.2 Pricing Process Framework

The Pricing Framework represents the four core competencies (Figure 1.1) that form the backbone of a science-based pricing framework. While the correct data infrastructure and processes enable the retailer to make sure data is available for

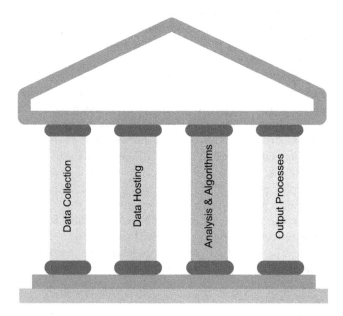

Figure 1.1 Pricing Process Framework.

use, the processes inside the organisation ensure that the pricing is connected to the everyday functioning of the retail organisation.

This section will deal with the infrastructure, management process, tools, and data required in the pricing analytical framework.

1.2.1 Data Collection

Collecting retail data entails learning about the performance of the physical business as well as clients' demographics, behaviours, attitudes, and activities. In order to better serve their consumers' requirements and increase sales, retailers could utilise this data to customise their purchasing, marketing, and price decisions.

1.2.1.1 POS Systems

A point of sale, sometimes known as a POS, is a machine that handles retail customers' transactions. A POS system includes a cash register. In today's world, Electronic POS terminals that can process cash, credit cards, and debit cards have essentially taken the place of traditional cash registers. In a physical store or at the cash register of an online retailer, a POS system is present without the actual register. Retailers can track pricing accuracy, gather marketing data, and keep track of inventory/ purchasing trends thanks to the increasingly sophisticated POS software solutions.

The POS system, in essence, acts as the hub where many data points – including sales, inventory management, payment processing, and customer management – merge to form the main source of data for analysis at a retail organisation.

The modern POS system can provide the following functionalities:

- Sales reports (based on product, hour, employee, the total cost of items sold, total retail amount, net profit, profit percentage, and gross margin)
- Brief summaries and graphs of the store's sales
- Digitally scan and count the products through the sales process
- Control inventory by developing product variations (size, colour)
- Assign each item in the inventory a special serial number
- Setting custom reorders of best-sellers to occur automatically
- Keep a record of the purchases made by clients
- Connect with customer loyalty systems
- Connect with customer communication management systems

1.2.1.2 Inventory and Logistics

Carrying the right amount of inventory is one of the lowest-hanging opportunities when it comes to leveraging analytics to increase retail profitability. To predict future demand, an inventory management system uses historical data and data analytics. More specifically, efficient inventory management software can analyse historical sales data and forecast future inventory demand by taking lead times and seasonality into account. Accurate demand forecasting is now achievable because of sophisticated inventory and sales management systems, which make it easier to balance product availability versus projected market demand than in the past.

In addition, visibility into the Logistics or Supply Chain of the order management system can enhance the accuracy of ordering and determine the right inventory levels for retail operations. For example, the total inventory carried is a combination of inventory in stock, on order and in transit.

1.2.1.3 IoT Devices

Retailers may improve the customer experience and increase conversions with the use of smart devices and/or Internet of Things (IoT) devices, which changes how day-to-day operations are carried out in stores. Among the benefits of using IoT in the retail industry are energy management, theft prevention, in-store navigation, and consumer interaction. Over the past several years, this particular segment of the industry has undergone major transformations because of technologies like big data management and artificial intelligence.

Industrial sensors for in-store data gathering, real-time analytical tools, and connected systems that combine the online and offline spheres of customer involvement are just a few examples of the numerous areas of the industry where retail IoT applications are used.

Some examples of IoT in retail are listed below:

- Collecting and sharing of data: Retail IoT devices, products, and environments may gather crucial information about the full product and shopping lifecycle using sensors. When this data is processed and evaluated, it yields insightful knowledge that aids retail management in making choices and enhancing operations and customer service.
- Data about the temperature and humidity of the stored goods may be transmitted in real-time to estimate the shelf life and freshness of the stored goods. These systems may be configured to take corrective merchandising actions and eventually reduce unwanted food waste.

1.2.1.4 Market Data Sources

Retailers can also leverage additional data from the market to make better-merchandising decisions. Here are six essential categories of marketing intelligence data that are generally available to the retailer.

Demographics: It's essential to identify the general customer information by collecting demographic information such as age, gender, and household income in order to get a complete picture of the audience as a whole. This data can be collected either at an aggregated level or at an individual level while making sure no privacy laws are violated legally and morally.

Purchase Behaviour: Some of the finest data available for what matters for future analysis and actions that might be taken comes from gathering information about what items were purchased, when and by whom and at what price. The typical systems available for collecting this data are different for the physical stores and the online stores.

Online Behaviour: For retailers wanting to engage audiences online. A customer who is visiting their website online can provide a wealth of additional information. However, we suggest care should be exercised to respect the privacy concern of their customers and also to respect the privacy laws in the region in which they operate.

Media Engagement: The most basic engagement data that marketers have access to may also be the most useful. The best and most readily available information about what customers want and expect from a brand is pretty much contained in those clicks, likes, shares, and email opens (or lack thereof).

Web Analytics: Beyond clicks and openings, audience behaviour on a brand's website also reveals important information about what is working and what needs improvement. This allows retailers to pinpoint exactly how audiences are consuming a website and then clarify that path.

Keyword Data: Paid search keyword data is a great way to improve upcoming campaigns and make adjustments to ongoing initiatives, but it's also a great way to find out what particular audiences want from a brand. These insights support the generation of both the most effective and efficient traffic.

1.2.1.5 Competitive Data

Data from the competition can be used to determine the position a retailer holds in the market. When retail deals with commoditised products such as milk and eggs, it becomes even more important for the retailer to have a price that is considered fair by the consumer. Especially on image items where customers remember the price of the products, it becomes even more important for a retailer to track the prices its competitor chooses for the same product. Using metrics such as the Competitive Price Indices (CPIs), retailers need to be aware of where they stand in the market and how these indices have changed over time. The use of competitive data is further discussed in Chapter 8 of the book.

1.2.2 Data Hosting

The act of keeping data on a dependable and reachable platform is known as data hosting. Although there isn't a set format for delivering this service, data hosting does demand a substantial investment and commitment. This becomes a long-term infrastructure that becomes a platform for many processes, analyses, and algorithms.

While data can be hosted on internal servers and systems as it has been done traditionally, retailers today also have the option of using a hosting service. A hosting service is a business that stores data for clients that lack the necessary storage space or require more storage space for their existing data. Typically, hosting services are offered through servers housed in data centres, where they are protected from outside attacks.

1.2.2.1 Data Lakes

Data lakes, as seen in Figure 1.2, are the perfect way to house all of retail's historical data because they can reasonably store a lot of data. A data lake's role is straightforward and scalable, giving businesses more affordable storage alternatives than other systems. Using a data lake allows companies that store enormous volumes of data – sometimes in petabytes – to reduce their data storage costs significantly. Because data lakes maintain all data in its original format, retailers can send the data through ETL (extract, transform, and load) pipelines later, once retailers are certain of the queries they want to run, without worrying about prematurely removing essential details.

Data is accessible throughout the firm due to a data lake, which serves as a central repository for the retailers' data. Data silos are produced when data is stored in separate databases. Data lakes dismantle these compartments and provide access to historical data analysis, allowing every department to use the same data to gain a deeper understanding of their clients. Retailers may fuel various activities, such as business intelligence, big-data analytics, data archiving, machine learning, and data science, by merging all of the data into a data lake.

1.2.2.2 Cloud vs On-Premise

A cloud environment differs significantly from an on-premises infrastructure in several key ways. What you need and what you're looking for in a solution will determine which approach is best for your business.

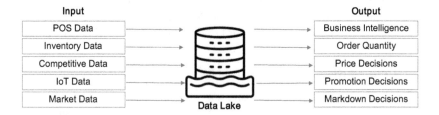

Figure 1.2 Data Lake.

1 Deployment
   On-Premises: In an on-premises environment, resources are set up internally and inside an organisation's IT infrastructure. A business is in charge of managing the solution and all of the processes connected to it.
      Cloud: Although there are several types of cloud computing, including public, private, and hybrid models, in a public cloud computing environment, resources are hosted on the premises of the service provider, but businesses can access and use as much of those resources as they need at any given time.

2 Cost
   On-Premises: Businesses that install software locally pay the continuing costs of the server hardware, electricity use, and space.
      Cloud: Businesses who use a cloud computing model only have to pay for the resources they use; they don't have to cover any maintenance or upkeep fees, and the cost changes according to how much is used.

3 Control
   On-premises: In a setting where data is stored on-site, businesses retain all of their information and have complete control over what happens to it, for better or worse. Due to this, businesses in highly regulated industries with elevated privacy concerns are more likely to wait to adopt cloud computing before their competitors.
      Cloud: Many businesses – and vendors, for that matter – have wrestled with the issue of data ownership in a cloud computing environment. Your third-party supplier stores data and encryption keys, therefore, you might not be able to access that data if the unexpected occurs and there is downtime.

4 Security
   On-Premises: Organisations that handle particularly sensitive data, such as those in the banking and government sectors, are required to have the level of protection and privacy that an on-premises environment offers. Despite the cloud's potential, security is a major concern for many companies, so even with some of its limitations and cost, an on-premises system makes more sense.
      Cloud: The biggest obstacle to adopting cloud computing continues to be security concerns. Cloud security breaches have been widely reported, and this has worried IT organisations all around the world. The hazards to security range from employee personal information like login credentials to the theft of intellectual property.

5 Compliance
   On-Premises: Regardless of the industry, many businesses nowadays operate under some kind of regulatory oversight. Although the Family Educational Rights and Privacy Act (FERPA), which contains comprehensive student records, and other governmental and industry regulations are among the others, HIPAA, which protects private health information, is arguably the most well-known. It is crucial for businesses that are subject

to these requirements to maintain compliance and always be aware of where their data is.

Cloud: Businesses that adopt a cloud computing model must exercise due diligence to confirm that their third-party supplier complies with all applicable legal requirements and industry standards. Customers, partners, and employees must have their privacy protected, and sensitive data must be secured.

1.2.2.3 ETL Processes

ETL consists of three steps:

1 Extraction: Getting data from one or more sources is the process of extraction. Documents, spreadsheets, CSV files, flat files, relational databases like Oracle, MySQL, SQL Server, non-relational databases, and more are examples of sources that can have various formats and organisational structures. Full and partial extraction are the two primary forms.

   • Full extraction is used for initial extractions or when the amount of data and ensuing extraction time are appropriate.
   • When it is unnecessary to extract all the data once more or when the volume of information is so large that a complete extraction is impractical, partial extraction is advised. Only updated or new data will be extracted in a partial extraction.

     The availability and integrity of the data are two additional factors that must be considered when deciding whether to perform a full or partial extraction. It implies that data that might result in an integrity error won't be evaluated for extraction until all transactions have been finished – for instance, a 10-question online test to gauge an engineer's understanding. The extraction process can only read the questions from complete tests if an engineer is midway through the trial and has already answered a few questions but has yet to finish. An integrity flaw might result from it.

2 Transformation: After the data has been extracted, we can start the transformation process by cleaning, manipulating, and transforming the data in accordance with technical specifications and business rules to maintain an acceptable level of data quality. A staging area could be required, depending on a variety of variables. A staging area is a temporary storage location used to house data extracted from data sources before it is transformed. Staging areas are only required in some projects, usually those with little data, but they are used in most projects. Various tasks are carried out during the transition period, including:

   • Selection: criteria for selecting the retrieved data. The decision might be made in either or both extraction and transformation processes.

- Integration: Data from the extraction phase are combined in the staging area through integration. Adding, removing, and updating data in the staging area based on the extracted data are all possible with this combination.
- Join: Similar to SQL joins, joins are used to connect extracted data (inner join, left join, right join, full join, etc.)
- Cleaning: To improve data quality, cleansing or scrubbing removes inconsistent, incorrect, or inaccurate data. When working with various data sources, the likelihood of encountering data issues that require cleaning increases.
- Summarising: condensing data collections for later usage
- Aggregation: Data gathered and compiled into aggregates.
- Consolidation: Data from several sources or organisational structures are combined to form a single data set.

3   Loading: Last but not least, loading the data into the destination is the ETL process's final step. Loading is the process of adding converted data to the repository, which is often a data warehouse database, whether it comes from a staging area or not. Data loading can be divided into three categories: complete or initial, incremental, and refresh.

- Full or original refers to the full set of data that has been extracted and modified. To prepare it for business users, all of the data in the staging area will be loaded into the destination.
- When loading data incrementally, only fresh data is loaded after comparing transformed data to the data at the end destination. Refresh load, which is described below, can be utilised in conjunction with the incremental load.
- In order to reflect changes made in the original source, data in the final destination must be refreshed. An update may be complete or gradual.

In conclusion, every retailer, regardless of size, can use ETL processes to integrate information that already exists and to produce an even greater wealth of information for decision-making, transforming data that was not previously usable into a new source of revenue.

1.2.3 Analysis and Algorithms

These days, data analysis is used more by major retail players around the world at every stage of the retail process. Examples include keeping track of newly popular products, forecasting sales and demand using predictive simulation, and optimising product and offer placements using heat maps of customers. With this, data analytics deals with identifying customers who, based on their prior purchases, would probably be interested in certain products, finding the best way to deal with them via targeted marketing strategies, and then determining what to sell next.

In today's market, consumers have lesser brand loyalty than ever before to any single retailer. Consumers are willing to switch to value and convenience which is provided by the most innovative retailer. The most successful retailers are continuously evolving their offerings and business model to suit the rapidly changing needs of their customers. Often times these decisions are supported by processing large amounts of data through algorithms to make choices on products, prices, discounts, and shipping channels.

1.2.3.1 Ordering Algorithms

The sales data captured by the POS systems and on the data infrastructure can be used to determine which products are most likely to catch on, where there is a need for potential new products, and to optimise pricing so that the retailer maintains a competitive edge. Customers use their own set of channels and applications to make decisions on the source, quantity, and quality of the products they want to buy as well as the appropriate price to pay for them. Most customers have a well-defined and sometimes subconscious thought process that helps them with decision-making.

Order Quantity: For the majority of retailers, forecast and replenishment order management is handled by set, rule-based inventory management systems. The goal is to develop a replenishment strategy that will reduce your ordering, holding, and shortage costs while considering the distribution of demand. The inventory formula, one example of how the required inventory quantity is determined, is shown in Figure 1.3.

In Figure 1.3, Q stands for Order Quantity and B_D stands for Base Demand.

Assortment Analysis: Retailers can get a broad picture of their whole market segment via assortment analysis. Assortment analysis can be used to identify the health of the assortment, increase or decrease product offerings based on product features relevant to each segment of the market, discontinue less efficient products, and also to allocate the space inside the store to maximise profits.

1.2.3.2 Pricing and Merchandising Algorithms

Having the right price for each product is crucial both for the retailer's profitability and the customer's satisfaction. While a price that is too low might drive the retailer out of business for lack of profits, a price too high will undoubtedly

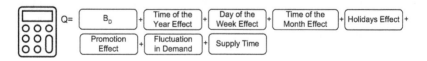

Figure 1.3 Inventory Formula.

drive the customer out of the store, again resulting in the retailer going out of business. Subsequent chapters of this book will cover the details of how pricing can be performed based on a combination of science and experience that can result in happy customers and successful retailers.

1.2.4 Output Processes

The purpose of the infrastructure, data analysis and algorithms should be to help make better retail merchandising and operating decisions. While past data analysis is oftentimes one of the best places to start the analytical journey, this slowly progresses towards prediction, optimisation, and eventually real-time execution of merchandising actions.

1.2.4.1 Business Intelligence

Retail business intelligence (BI) can be defined as the process of transforming data into insights in the retail sector. There are several ways to accomplish this, but generally speaking, analytics are used to spot trends and patterns. BI can assist retailers in making wiser decisions about inventory, pricing, marketing, and other factors. Retailers can now leverage a variety of various technologies to enhance their BI. These consist of:

- Data analysis
- Analytics for text
- Predictive modelling
- Using predictive analytics
- Graphical displays and dashboards

It is crucial for merchants to choose the appropriate tools for their particular needs because each of these solutions has its own special advantages. By deciding which metrics to track in order to obtain the information they require, retailers can also get the most from these solutions. This is further discussed in detail in Chapter 6 of the book.

1.2.4.2 KPI Monitoring

A KPI, or key performance indicator, is a defined and quantifiable metric used to evaluate the effectiveness of a retail operation. These performance indicators can be utilised in a number of ways to track and monitor retail performance. It will take continual work and dedication to monitor a store's KPIs, but the potential rewards are well worth it. The meticulously gathered data will first reveal new problems that demand the retailer's attention. If the retailer responds promptly, they might be able to "tweak" their way to a resolution before the problem escalates to the point where management must intervene with "all hands on deck". It's important to respond quickly when the retailer notices a KPI trending in the wrong direction to reduce its detrimental financial impact. In other words, retailers can identify the issue before small losses turn into a flood of money leaving the company. Finally, keep in mind that the retail business doesn't run entirely independently. Most of the time, rival businesses are all around the retailers, each vying for a larger portion of the market or sales. Monitoring the KPIs is critical to maintaining (or enhancing) the store's competitive position.

For instance, tracking sales per square foot and sales per employee on a monthly basis makes it possible to see trends and make changes very quickly. On the other hand, it makes sense to track the stock turn rates on a seasonal and annual basis. The nature of foot traffic is distinct. Reviewing data on a weekly, monthly, or even annual basis can reveal trends in the business of the store.

1.2.4.3 Promotion/Price Execution

With the right infrastructure for data in place, new processes can be defined to achieve a pricing framework.

An example of how this pricing process is built for a large convenience store chain is shown in Figure 1.4.

1.2.4.4 Compliance Checking

Retail compliance is the practice of each store adhering to corporate headquarters' rules for procedures and presentation in order to uphold a consistent corporate standard throughout all stores. For instance, observing corporate standards for displays, advertising signage, store layout, cleanliness, and safety protocols would be included in retail compliance. Further compliance with the price and promotions,

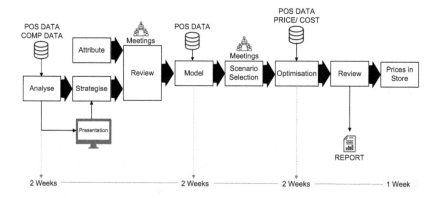

Figure 1.4 Example of a Convenience Store's Pricing Process.

meaning the stores are actually displaying and selling at the price points as directed by the corporate headquarters is critical in ensuring the desired strategy is actually being implemented.

1   Auditing: A store audit is a thorough examination intended to ascertain whether rules, regulations, and practices are effective and where staff members may enhance operations at the store level.
2   Robots: The use of in-store robots to assist a major retailer with compliance issues is one of the most well-known cases of robotics in retail. To help ensure availability, proper shelf placement, and price accuracy, automated shelf-scanning robots are being added to move down store aisles and scan items on store shelves.
3   Scan Data: Verifying scan data against the desired strategy can highlight many inconsistencies that need to be addressed. Examples of this could be incorrect prices, incorrect promotions, scanning products that are already discontinued, and detecting situations of products with zero sales even though they could be in stock.

1.2.4.5 Real-Time Execution

Retailers have the capacity to develop, carry out, and enhance pricing and advertising actions in real time. Cheaper and more advanced technologies enable retailers to collect and process vast amounts of data in real-time and advanced artificial intelligence algorithms can make automated decisions that can be implemented at a product-store level. While on the one hand, a retailer would need the ability to collect, process, and automate the decision-making process, on the other hand, the retailer will also need the ability to execute these decisions in real-time as well. Some decisions such as ordering can be done via software, and other decisions such as price and promotions will need additional hardware components such as Electronic Shelf Labels (ESLs), In-Store Displays or even directly on Customer Devices such as Cell Phones, or Smart Carts.

1   ESL: ESLs give retailers the ability to instantly adjust pricing across the whole shop without having to spend days on tiresome and error-prone manual work. Retailers may improve click and collect, improve pricing efficiency and accuracy, and streamline replenishment with ESLs. Store owners may easily synchronise pricing to keep up with the online competition and respond swiftly to market prices. A seamless in-store and online buying experience with price transparency are made possible by ESLs, which gives customers the ability to see the correct price right away and receive customised, in-depth product information. This topic is discussed in section 1.4.6 in greater detail.
2   In-store Displays: Retailers today have many points of displays that are electronic and can be controlled in real-time inside the retail stores. These include TV monitors, digital signage, smart refrigerator with electronic

displays, check-out screens, and even speakers connected with automatic announcement capabilities.

3   Customer Devices: Customers carry cell phones which can be leveraged to collect data on movement, traffic, and customer behaviour and also to supply information such as discounts, product recommendations, and directions/store maps. Customers might also get access to other devices while inside the store such as Smart Carts or scan guns that can be leveraged to both collect useful data and supply relevant information to the customers.

1.3 Strategic Pricing Framework

While pricing is a critical function that math can help solve for an "optimal" solution, it is important to consider the various strategic goals, business rules, and constraints in the overall pricing process. (Figure 1.5).

Some of these factors include

- Profit/bottom line
- Price image/customer perception
- Vendor relationships
- Private label growth
- Competitive strategy
- Market share

1.3.1 Profit/Bottom Line

The profit from the operations of a retail organisation remains one of the primary goals for a pricing framework. This profit eventually determines the success or failure of an organisation and it is essential the retail organisation remains focused on profit to ensure its own survival and eventually to serve the needs of its customers.

1.3.2 Price Image/Customer Perception

Price perception refers to a customer's perception of how expensive or economical a retailer is in the mind of the consumer. The perception is driven by a

Figure 1.5 Strategic Pricing Framework.

combination of factors such as the actual prices of products that a customer might remember, the look and feel of the entire store or the ambience of the store, comparison of the prices to other available options for a consumer and also the marketing and advertising messaging used by the retailer.

Retailers can aim to build a perception of providing a better value for their customers by addressing each of these factors above through science-based merchandising actions, building KPIs to measure the perceptions and reacting appropriately to achieve the desired perception.

1.3.3 Vendor Relationships

A buyer-supplier or vendor relationship is crucial to business continuity. It is critical to ensure quality and maintain a continuous and profitable supply of products that needs to be sold in a retail store. While a vendor is looking to sell his most profitable products through the retailer, the retailer has to balance between carrying profitable products, ensuring the availability of essential products, building the desired image amongst its consumers, and also running promotions that increase the overall sales of the store and not just those of the promoted products.

1.3.4 Private Label Products

Retailers leverage private label products to sell more profitable products in their assortment as a substitute for national label products. By having suitable arrangements with low-cost suppliers or local manufacturing facilities, retailers can produce similar products as popular brands at a much lower cost since they do not have to pay for additional costs such as shipping and marketing. Then by applying their own labels on the products, the brand name the customer is already familiar with and trusts, retailers are able to fulfil the needs of their customers at a much lower price and higher profit margins.

Given these incentives, retailers often need pricing strategies that will increase the sales of private-label products. This can be done by making sure there is an appropriate price gap between a private label product and its comparative national label product. The retailer will also need to study the assortment and changing demands closely to ensure that the right type of private-label products is being introduced into the assortment consistently.

1.3.5 Competitive Strategy

Retailing often time involves selling products that are classified as commodities. It is often very little, or no differentiation between the same product sold by different retailers, and the consumers are likely to choose from the retailer offering the best value for the product. One of the major factors of this value in the consumer's mind is indeed the price of the product, but not the only factor; other factors such as convenience, assortment depth, and ambience also play an important role.

Retailers should determine how they should be positioning themselves in the marketplace and what price they should be selling each of their products and ideally this should be done by location or by zone. A scientific analysis of historical data can reveal several important factors, such as competitive intensity by store location, most price-sensitive products, and current competitive position.

A strategic goal must be determined based on the analysis of these factors to determine the right competitive and pricing strategy that needs to be executed.

1.3.6 Market Share

A company's market share is the percentage of total revenues in its target market. Market share is measured by dividing a company's sales made during a certain period by the industry's total sales made over the same period. A company that expands its market share will also expand its revenues more quickly than its competitors. A larger market share often delivers better marketing expenditure returns and better negotiation power with vendors that can result in higher margins and also lower operating costs on a unit basis. Thus, a company's market share is an important measure of its success in the market.

In certain cases, retailers might choose to pursue revenue or market share instead of profit, almost always only for a certain duration of time. This is especially true when entering new markets or if the strategy is to gain market share against competitors. It might be necessary in some cases to sacrifice profits to obtain market share. However, with an analytics-based approach, retailers can target a balanced growth scenario where they could achieve positive numbers for both market share and profit at the same time. It is important to analyse which markets and categories are ideal for increasing market share and where a profit goal can be prioritised.

1.4 Pricing Organisation Structure

Companies may establish a strategic pricing organisation by focusing on four key elements: structure, decision rights and influence, skills and capabilities, and scale. Companies that establish strategic pricing organisations will undoubtedly gain an advantage over competitors.

Let us look at some of the key roles and skills that are typical for the pricing function in a retail organisation.

- Vice President of Merchandising: A strong management team is required to manage and guide employees and lead the company with the right strategy for the retailer. A vice president is responsible for executing the operations of the retailer in line with the strategic objectives as set by the Organisation.

- Director of Pricing: Oftentimes, large retail organisations assign one Director for each retail category so that the strategic goals of the category can be managed effectively. Smaller organisations might have multiple categories assigned to one Director.
- Pricing Manager: A pricing manager manages a team of pricing analysts to determine the prices for each product location, audit the prices and measure the performance of the prices.
- Pricing Analyst: A Pricing Analyst is usually knowledgeable about a smaller segment of the category and keeps a close eye on factors such as margin, market share and competitive prices. The analysts are well-versed in data analysis and presentation skills.
- Technology Team: The Technology team consists of employees that help the pricing organisation leverage the data required to perform the pricing functions. This includes data storage, extraction and building of data tables and structures that feed into the pricing algorithms and applications.
- Analytics Team: Larger retail organisations often have an in-house analytics team that is in charge of data mining and providing insights often through the Business Intelligence (BI) platforms that help the pricing teams make everyday decisions.
- Pricing Solution Providers: Retailers often have to rely upon external vendors and consultants to provide complementary solutions needed for the effective functioning of the retailer's pricing organisation.

Some of the potential resources are listed below:

- Retail Strategy Consultant
- Business/Pricing Analysts
- Data Engineers
- Algorithm Developers
- Application Developers
- Category Managers

1.4.1 Retail Strategy Consultant

A retail strategy consultant brings expertise from working with best practices at different retail organisations into the retail organisation. Strategy consultants can play a key role in establishing data structures, analytical frameworks and pricing processes to help the retailer become successful in the marketplace.

An experienced retail strategy consultant can leverage data to provide strategic input in setting the goals and objectives for each category.

1.4.2 Business/Pricing Analysts

A Business Analyst, or Pricing Analyst, collects data about a company's operations to improve its systems and processes. The analyst researches business processes, provides recommendations to company management, and also analyses the impact of those recommendations.

An external business analyst is technically savvy in using the tools and techniques relevant to the retailer's pricing needs but might not be familiar with the intricacies of the retailer's business operations such as vendor relationships. The external business/pricing analysts work in conjunction with the retailer's own pricing analysts and other resources.

1.4.3 Data Engineers

A data engineer is an IT professional whose primary job is to prepare data for analytical or operational uses. External data engineers are well-versed in bringing together multiple data streams to prepare them for use with the pricing tools, processes and algorithms.

1.4.4 Algorithm Developers

Algorithm developers have become an integral part of innovations in computer science. They create and fix code by employing logic and reasoning. The specialised algorithm developers might only need to work for a few weeks to develop powerful algorithms for the retailer's pricing needs. However, these algorithm developers are expensive and often thrive well in continuously challenging environments. These resources are best leveraged as external suppliers for most retail organisations.

1.4.5 Application Developers

An application developer is a critical part of the technical and/or project management team responsible for ensuring user needs are met through the software deployed. Working in teams, they help deploy releases to internal or external clients. Many application developers work on a contract basis for companies. Application development is a collaborative process, and many work in teams with others to design, develop, and program applications or software.

They understand client requirements and create new applications, creatively design prototypes according to specifications, write high-quality source code for programs, and perform unit and integration testing before launching the application.

1.4.6 Category Managers

Category managers play a key role in the development and success of a product or service within a retail organisation. They manage the product category and are responsible for the pricing and overall promotion of that product or service.

They understand consumer needs and the retail environment. They possess knowledge of marketing and sales principles.

A category manager analyses data to gain insights, meets suppliers/retailers to discuss plans, briefs market research companies, and updates category reports. They help in new product development (NPD) or promotions, reviewing the retailer's planogram (POG) – that is, its model for displaying merchandise.

Category managers analyse data to determine industry and consumer trends. They devise long-term development strategies for product categories. They develop exit strategies for unsuccessful products and foster trust relationships with vendors to achieve better pricing and quality of services. They help place appropriate orders to ensure product availability that meets consumer demands and determine the positioning of a product category to maximise visibility. They even liaise with marketing teams to determine competitive pricing and promotional activities of a product category.

1.5 Hardware Requirements

To make their business more efficient and profitable, many retailers have made successful investments in store-based hardware for data collection. Some of these are shown in Figure 1.6:

- Smart cameras
- Traffic counters
- Inventory sensors
- Smart refrigerators
- IoT devices/sensors
- Electronic shelf labels
- Smart digital displays
- Beacons/proximity sensors
- Smart carts

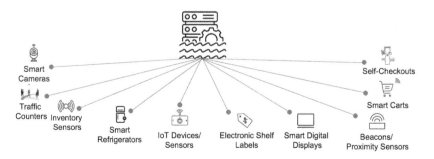

Figure 1.6 In-Store Retail Hardware.

1.5.1 Smart Cameras

A smart camera is a hardware device that can help the retailer track the presence and behaviour of its customers. The cameras often have technologies that can help them detect important information such as traffic, demographics of the customers, their mood, and shopping behaviour and also detect real-time theft or altercations.

1.5.2 Traffic Counters

Traffic counters track the entry/exit of visitors in a retail store using counting sensors. These devices can be enabled with thermal imaging systems, smart-flooring technologies, Wi-Fi trackers, manual clickers, or infrared beams. These devices provide actionable analytics data to measure conversion rates and create shop layouts and window displays. These can also be useful in staff allocation and in identifying customer pathways to help with pricing and merchandising decisions.

1.5.3 Inventory Sensors

Retailers can deploy inventory sensors that can detect how many products are placed on a shelf or tray and when it is out of stock. These sensors can provide real-time alerts to both the retail headquarters and the store managers so that prompt action can be taken to correct a potential stock out or low inventory situation. When used in conjunction with inventory management systems, these sensors can enhance the accuracy of inventory management in especially challenging categories such as fresh produce.

1.5.4 Smart Refrigerators

A smart refrigerator, commonly referred to as an internet refrigerator, can communicate with the internet. This type of refrigerator can detect when a food item needs replenishment. Retailers can increase operational efficiency with dynamic inventory management and earn more revenue with data-driven stocking and selling.

1.5.5 IoT Devices/Sensors

The IoT is a network of physical objects (things) that are embedded with sensors, software, and other technologies to connect and exchange data with other devices and systems over the internet. The retail applications where these devices can be used are personalised retail marketing and content delivery, staffing-level indicators, temperature monitoring, humidity monitoring, cashier payment systems, movement-tracking systems for optimal store setup, IoT-enabled warehouse robots, wireless shipment tracking devices, real-time monitoring of goods, and inventory management tools.

1.5.6 Electronic Shelf Labels

Retailers use electronic shelf label (ESL) technology to showcase product prices on shelves. When a price is modified under the supervision of a central server, the product pricing is automatically updated within seconds. Electronic display modules are often mounted on the front edge of shop shelves. In addition to product pricing, ESLs can be used in building signs, shelf space, and even in the manufacturing process.

The ESL market is anticipated to develop steadily at a compound annual growth rate (CAGR) of more than 16%. The retail business accounts for the bulk of ESL users. These businesses include grocery stores, hardware stores, sports equipment, furniture, consumer appliances, and electrical/electronic gadget retailers, among others. This expected rise is attributable to the retail industry's rising use of ESL now that it has become cost-effective. Europe – with its high presence of local and multinational shops, dominates the ESL industry in terms of size. Thereby accounting for almost one-third of the overall market share in the year 2017. The market in the Asia Pacific (APAC), on the other hand, is anticipated to develop at the fastest CAGR over the forecast period. According to Markets and Markets Reports 2021, the market for ESL is anticipated to reach USD 2,092 million by 2026 at a CAGR of 20.4% from an estimated value of USD 826 million in 2021.

1.5.6.1 Benefits of ESL

ESL technology brings many benefits to the retail business. Price management-labour expenses are reduced, pricing accuracy is improved, and dynamic pricing is made possible. Dynamic pricing allows retailers to adjust prices in response to demand, online competition, inventory levels, item shelf life and promotions. The following are some of the other benefits.

1   Accurate Pricing: Using a link between the in-store point-of-sale processor and the label management software, prices on shelves are updated on demand and on time to match price files on the label management software. This provides pricing accuracy and helps avoid price integrity-related branding concerns.
2   Saves Costs: Employees need not print labels and manually replace them in the shelf tags when prices are altered and updated – as they would with standard pricing labels. As all changes are done in the label management software and digitally updated to the labels, ESL removes the need to visit

each shelf and make adjustments. This saves merchants money on materials and labour when creating and changing printed tags – giving them the option to change pricing on the go.

3   Product Finder: Retailers can link each ESL tag with an external application to provide navigation capabilities for their items. Thus, customers can locate a producer either through a retailer-developed mobile application or through an external digital signature that directs them to the product's location.

4   In-Store Heat Map: Some ESL providers interface with Bluetooth-equipped low-energy using devices to measure consumer movement and how long they stay in a spot. This is accomplished by presenting a picture of the store's floor plan on the label management software, along with a heat map indicating the locations of hot spots based on Bluetooth replies from high-traffic regions.

5   Control Inventory Levels: Inventory control is critical for retailers. It can be shown on an ESL using a link with the point-of-sale processor. The ESL can provide an estimated date by when goods on the shelf need to be replenished. It can also show a fast response code allowing customers to quickly discover the item online or merchants to provide customers with the required product information.

1.5.6.2 Disadvantages of ESL

While ESL has its advantages, it also has certain drawbacks, as follows:

1   Error Propagation: As ESL is regulated by label management software, any incorrect or undervalued pricing placed into the label management software will be reflected across the entire retail chain.

2   Inability to estimate the ROI: Due to the enormous number of ESL that a retailer would need for its locations, the initial investment cost for a store may be more than expected. This, along with the difficulty to measure any increase in the customer experience after ESL deployment, makes calculating the return on investment (ROI) challenging.

1.5.6.3 Companies Providing ESL

Some of the companies that provide ESL services are as follows:

• Displaydata Ltd.: Provides good quality and an affordable total cost of ownership. It also provides superior in-store scalability and engagement. The pricing is intelligent, and profits are good. Altierre Corp.: Provides wireless dynamic pricing solutions for retail chains.
• SES-imagotag: It is a global pioneer in the field and a digital solutions expert for physical retail. It provides an improved in-shop experience and manages stores with laser-like accuracy.

- SoluM (Samsung): Provides solutions to sketch out a strategy. Its solutions are based on advanced technologies and effective operations, and quality control.

1.5.7 Smart Digital Displays

Digital pictures, videos, websites, weather data, restaurant menus, and text are displayed on Smart Digital Displays. The technologies used include liquid crystal display (LCD), light emitting diode (LED), projection, and e-paper. These are used for navigation, exhibits, marketing, and outdoor advertising in retail establishments. In addition, these technologies improve the in-store experience by delivering targeted advertising – related to the products customers are shopping for. These displays keep customers informed about the latest product news and promotions. This is done by delivering information directly to buyers in retail locations.

1.5.8 Beacons/Proximity Sensors

A beacon/proximity sensor detects the presence of adjacent objects without making direct contact. A proximity sensor often produces an electromagnetic field or a beam of electromagnetic radiation – for example, infrared – and monitors the field or return signal for changes. Retailers may use data from beacons to estimate when customers enter or exit a location or when they are loitering around a certain area. These sensors can be used to create context-aware applications, such as tailored advertising, useful product information, and even improved shop layouts.

The success of beacon technology is related to the increased use of smartphones in retail stores. Some estimates show that digital interactions now affect 56 cents of every dollar spent in brick-and-mortar businesses in some countries.

1.5.8.1 Benefits of Beacons/Proximity Sensors

- Increase the Granularity of Customer Data: Data can be collected using beacons in shopping floor areas with the highest and least foot traffic. These sensors can track the movement of employees on the sales floor, and in stock rooms, levels of customer involvement with various retail categories/items, information on new and returning customers, and resource use in-store and across the supply chain. Retailers can improve the usability of their shop premises by optimising stalls and merchandising layouts. They can cut down wait times at checkouts and other touch points using this diversified data.
- Enhance the Usefulness of Stores: Customers can be guided around a retail area by beacons, which can alleviate this logistical difficulty. Customers can just open the shop app and see where they are right now, search for the location of a certain item, and ask for directions.

- Proximity marketing as an Advantage: Sending promotional messages to passing consumers to encourage them to visit the business and make a purchase is one of the most common beacon use cases. These alerts can either be generic or act as an advertisement or they can be highly customised and match a customer's prior purchase history to the present visit. Customers can also be notified of in-store events, such as food tasting or a beauty demonstration, using beacons.
- Loyalty: In a store, most customers use their smartphones to get more information about items. As part of the loyalty program, retailers may take advantage of this behaviour and employ beacons to send promos. Customers feel like they are part of a community, establish confidence in the brand, and are more likely to choose it over the competition. Customers will also be more likely to download the store's application and use it in the store to obtain a discount, learn about related items, or enter a contest if they engage in a loyalty program.

1.5.8.2 Limitations of Beacons/Proximity Sensors

- Physical Restraints: Depending on the surrounding materials and proximity of other beacons, beacon signals can easily be reflected or absorbed. As a result, some areas of a business may become blind spots. These sensors may send out messages not relevant to the customer. Another point to consider is the timing of alerts. Some alerts may arrive with a delay due to changes in Bluetooth signal strength, killing their relevance and the general notion of a continuous experience.
- Considerations of Ethics: Care should be exercised so that the data being leveraged and used is done in compliance with both the interests and the legal requirements of the operating geography. Users appear to be more devoted to tailored messages sent via beacons with considerably greater open rates as compared to regular push notifications/alerts. However, before retailers can send a message through a beacon, they need to ensure that their application and Bluetooth are both turned on and the customer has given consent to receiving such messages.

1.5.8.3 Companies Providing Beacons

Following are some of the companies providing beacon services.

- RetailNext
- PlaceIQ
- Euclid Analytics
- SWIRL
- Beabloo

1.5.9 Smart Carts

A Smart shopping cart helps a customer perform shopping through scanning, product locating and payment functionalities. Smart shopping cart solutions don't require significant store upgrades. Instead of installing complex equipment across the whole business, smart shopping carts may be installed one at a time.

A retailer can leverage additional insights generated with the shopping cart such as customer route taken, time spent inside the store and decision-making time in each segment. This data becomes especially powerful when combined with customer loyalty and POS. Finally, the carts can also be used to deploy real-time coupons and promotions to increase sales and introduce relevant products to customers.

1.5.10 Self-Checkouts

Self-checkouts (SCOs), also known as assisted checkouts (ACOs) or self-service checkouts, are machines that allow customers to scan purchased goods themselves without doing a standard staffed checkout. Customers can scan item barcodes using SCOs, eliminating the need for one-on-one employee assistance. Self-checkouts are most commonly found in supermarkets. However, these are also used in department and convenience stores. Just one staff member may oversee many self-checkout stations, assisting customers with transactions, adjusting prices, and offering other services.

1.5.10.1 Benefits of Self-Checkouts

- Self-checkout terminals may be strategically positioned around a store, allowing customers to pay wherever they are. This cuts down on long queues at manned checkouts and the time customers spend in a store waiting to make payments.
- The staff can be redeployed to other duties more efficiently if self-checkout is applied. They can get more time to attend to customers.
- Customers may explore more and buy goods in-store and have them delivered or picked up later.
- Retailers may propose further purchases to customers during the checkout process using guided selling capabilities. For instance, when customers buy electronic items, retailers may give them an extended warranty.
- Customers can pay using an option of their convenience – with credit cards or by using their phones, among others.

1.5.10.2 Disadvantages of Self-Checkout

- Sometimes, the clients may be disappointed by a self-checkout machine that does not operate correctly. Though businesses can hire staff to troubleshoot as required to mitigate this potential issue. Additionally, retailers need to ensure a seamless customer experience by using easy-to-use technology.

- Some surveys indicate that about 4% (Palmer Retail Solutions) of store items scanned by self-checkout kiosks are not paid for. Although this figure is not much higher than other forms of theft. To counteract theft, store owners and operators can install visible security equipment on the storefront and hire vigilant workers to monitor the self-checkout area. Most thefts are deterred simply by the presence of workers.
- A common issue regarding self-checkout systems is that some staff may lose employment by rendering cashiers redundant. While this worry persists, several businesses have pledged to openly share their operational changes.

1.6 Conclusion

In this chapter, we noted what impact retail pricing could have on the overall profitability and success of a retail organisation. We also looked at several factors that are necessary to ensure a good pricing strategy and the resources needed to execute this strategy. While the end goal might be to have the perfect price for every product at any given time, the beginning could be something as simple as an excel analysis to understand the role each product plays in the overall strategy.

A well-defined and data-driven pricing process can enable retailers to leverage existing data to make streamlined decisions that generate incremental profit and market share while providing maximum value and satisfaction to their customers.

Chapter 2

Base Pricing

2.1 Introduction

Base Pricing is one of the most important functions of a retail organisation. It is, in essence, the price a customer will be paying for a product or service when it is not on promotion or clearance. Studies show that a 2% change in base prices can impact net margins by more than 10%. However, it is important to note that these prices need not be increased every time to achieve an increase in profit. Lower prices can result in increased profit as well.

It can also be observed that, that the right price creates a favourable image amongst the target customers, drives traffic to the store, helps maintain competitiveness, drives private label strategy, and also maintains healthy vendor relationships.

In this chapter, we will discuss the various aspects of the base pricing process. This includes the science of pricing itself, the strategic considerations, the details of a typical pricing process and methodologies to measure and maintain the pricing process. We will study the pricing structure, pricing zones, results measurement, price maintenance, and how retailers can build a process for efficient ongoing operations.

2.2 Pricing Strategy Formulation

The base price of a product is an important benchmark on which the retailers' operations stand. Not only does the most important part of the retailers' margins are generated from sales at the base price, but the base price also forms the basis on which promotion and markdown decisions are made. In this section we will take a look at some of the factors that play a role in the formulation of the strategy for base pricing.

2.2.1 Retail Pricing Strategies

Retailers can choose from many different strategies for retailing pricing. Before embarking on our journey to establish a pricing strategy and process let us take a look at the major pricing strategy types and initial considerations.

DOI: 10.4324/9781003382140-3

The three major pricing strategies used by retailers are shown below:

1 **Cost-Based Pricing:** Setting prices based on the costs by adding a markup price for products is one of the most common pricing strategies. Although easy to use and execute, this is also one of the most inefficient forms of pricing as the customer does not care for how much it costs to produce the product, the customer cares about the "value" of the product which is not a factor in the Cost-Based Pricing strategy.

2 **Market-Based Pricing:** A relatively more complex, but safe strategy in most cases is to simply use the price of the market or a market leader to establish pricing. This is especially relevant in an over-commoditised market where there is little differentiation in the product offering and convenience of the goods being purchased. For example, if three vendors are selling popcorn next to each other in a marketplace, it might be a good idea to match the price offered by the other vendors. However, care should be taken to not blindly match the prices of a competitor in retail as the cost structure for each retailer is different.

3 **Demand-Based Pricing:** Measuring the demand to establish the most optimal price for a customer can deliver profit and customer satisfaction at the same time. However, establishing this optimal price requires investment in data, processes and optimisation. Further, demand is estimated based on customer, location and time. Dynamic demand-based pricing may be employed for further efficiency in retail pricing.

2.2.2 Initial Considerations

While the long-term planning should include a full-fledged data infrastructure, defined pricing processes and tools to deliver demand-based pricing, below is a list of steps that can be undertaken to prepare ahead.

2.2.2.1 Outline the High-Level Pricing Strategy

Retailers can optimise sales and profits when the price, value proposition, positioning, and brand value are all in synchronisation with each other. If operational efficiency is the retailer's value proposition, the price could be competitive. A low price can also communicate the wrong message, especially if the value proposition is quality leadership.

2.2.2.2 Price Products to Meet Profit Goals

Pricing should be aligned with the profit goals set at the corporate level by the retailer. In some cases, the retailer's goal might be to achieve the maximum possible profit in a short amount of time and in others, the retailer's goal might be to forego the profit in exchange for a larger market share in the near term.

2.2.2.3 Examine Competitive Prices

It makes business sense to first compare prices and the market position of products and services offered by competitors before deciding on a final price. Based on this data, retailers should work on their pricing and plan their approach. It is important to consider pricing and positioning together as both are intertwined.

2.2.2.4 Examine Competitive Pricing Actions and Reactions

When competitors change their prices, a retailer needs to assess the market situation and consider many options before responding. Consider how the price shift has affected the market. Is the price change temporary? Is there a shift in the offering and/or customer segment? Is it really impacting the market share? This examination can help retailers in avoiding price matching that may not be necessary.

2.2.2.5 Determine a Single Customer's Profitability

One way to analyse the profitability of the offerings is by assessing the price and possible profitability for a single customer. This is especially useful when providing a unique product or service or a complex combination of bespoke items. To figure out the profitability, identify the costs incurred including overheads.

2.2.2.6 Understand Purchase Criteria

When a customer makes a purchase, they consciously or unconsciously assess the goods on several parameters or essential qualities. A customer may be price sensitive for a specific product or desire the highest quality at any cost on another product. In other cases, a customer might light a nice ambience or customer support in other cases, a customer might want to complete the purchase quickly with convenience. Thus, retailers need to know their customers well and the value they seek, this will help them price their products appropriately and promote goods or services accordingly. A customer can compare a range of items or services offered and assess them for their strengths and shortcomings before making a purchase. The main purchasing criteria or the characteristics that are most important to customers when making a purchase, or when choosing a product or service from one retailer over another are the following: Price, Quality, Service, Speed, Scale and Product Range.

2.2.3 Pricing Goals

A Strategic Pricing Goal should be a well-informed decision that forms the basis for the merchandising objectives for each category and markets a retailer operates in. While the main goal for a retailer might be profit, the strategic objective could be more focused such as achieving a certain market share or growth rate in a well-chosen market segment.

Setting clear goals to achieve can go a long way to help retailers set their pricing. Here are some ways for retailers to begin.

2.2.3.1 Increasing Market Share or Margins

This is one of the most important and also most common objectives with retailers. Increasing market share typically leads to increasing margins which is key to the success of any retailer.

2.2.3.2 Increasing Brand Awareness

With so many brands and goods to choose from, how can retailers stand out? Creating a compelling and engaging brand story allows customers to engage with the company on a more personal level. This is a good approach to establishing brand recall and awareness.

2.2.3.3 Increasing Brand Loyalty

Customer acquisition is not inexpensive. Acquiring new clients involves time, effort, and money. Brand loyalty not only ensures recurring purchases but also leads to additional benefits as loyal customers become brand ambassadors. Retailers get additional marketing mileage from their word-of-mouth recommendations, active referrals, live product displays, and so on. Customers' confidence and trust are required to establish brand loyalty. The ability to provide high-quality items on time and with excellent customer service is critical.

2.2.3.4 Increasing Customer Engagement

When retailers invest in customer engagement, retailers provide customers additional opportunities to interact with the brand, goods, fundamental values, and more. For example, retailers can make a prominent presence on social media. By making a year-long social media engagement schedule, retailers can commit to being more engaged on social media. Throughout the customer journey, retailers can identify and enhance the customer experience. Consider brand marketing events, product discovery, reviews, and customer service at check-out, among other things. These situations can occur both online and in-store.

2.2.3.5 Creating a Multi-Channel Presence

There's no better time than now to become an omnichannel store if retailers have not done that already. By allowing retailers to sell across as many outlets and channels as possible, an effective omnichannel retail strategy may help retailers increase sales. A lot of planning is required here. Combine and track inventory movement across the sales channels using an omnichannel inventory management solution. For example, if a customer purchases something online and wants to pick it up in a shop, an omnichannel system can determine which stores have the required item in stock. Additionally, retailers can help customers turn contemplation into conversion, by strategically utilising brand touchpoints to create a seamless experience.

2.2.3.6 Positioning

After retailers figure out who their target customer is and the desired image they wish to project, they will have to consider the positioning. What part of the market do retailers want to be in? Do the retailers want to be in the most expensive, luxury, high-end brand in the sector, be the most affordable one, or be somewhere in the middle?

2.2.4 Strategic Components

A company's retail pricing strategy is influenced by a variety of factors. To name a few: production cost, competition, brand and product value, price elasticity, profit margin, market share, and legal limitations. The considerations from the factors mentioned so far should help formulate a strategy for the Company, Competition and Private Label Products.

2.2.4.1 Company Strategy

The overall goal of the company mainly in terms of revenue, profit and market share goals are some of the vital components of a Company Level Retail Strategy. Some examples of Company Strategies that form the basis for a pricing organisation are as follows:

- Achieve 20% market share in high-end convenience retail in the Nordics.
- Become the #1 player for Vegan Meat in the Colorado market.
- Achieve 35% gross margins across the United States in 2 years.
- Introduce the brand into 2 new markets with a market share of 5%.

2.2.4.2 Competitive Strategy

The retail organisation should set a high-level strategy on what needs to be achieved with regard to the competition. This can vary based on the category or markets in which the retailer operates and any strategic decision should be based on analytics-based findings from the market-level data. A popular way to do this is by defining Competitive Price Indices (CPIs) and targeting for the CPIs. This can be done by groups of products in each market. Using the CPIs, retailers can set business goals such as:

- Maintain a CPI <0.90 for all Image Items in the US-North-Compete Zone.
- Maintain a CPI between 1.2 and 1.5 for all Profit Drivers in the US-South Zone.
- Maintain a CPI equal to 1.0 for all new product launches across the United States in Q1.

2.2.4.3 Private Label Strategy

Private labels form an important part of a retailer's assortment for many reasons. Retailers should define specific goals for the private label products in each market to achieve the goals set for the Private Label products. A definitive Private Label Strategy can be established and used as guidelines for the pricing process, some examples of Private Label Strategy can include:

- Grow market share for Private Labels to 25% in Baby Care.
- Ensure each corresponding private label product provides better value by at least 10%.
- Beat the matching private label product at a competitor by at least 10%.

2.3 Science of Base Pricing

Pricing a retail product is an art as well as a science. Retailers often price products based on experience and intuition which can be very effective. At the same time, the human brain is not capable of calculating the right price for each product by location at all points in time. Leveraging the power of data analysis and technology in conjunction with experience and intuition can provide a very powerful combination that can make retailing very successful.

In this section, we will explore a few key factors that are a part of any science-based pricing process. The implementation of analytics-based and statistical methods, such as economic modelling, programming, statistics, and econometrics is the science of base pricing. Figure 2.1 shows the various factors that play a role in pricing.

2.3.1 Price Elasticity and Cross Elasticity

The price elasticity of demand is the measurement of the ratio between the change in the consumption of a product and the change in its price. The cross

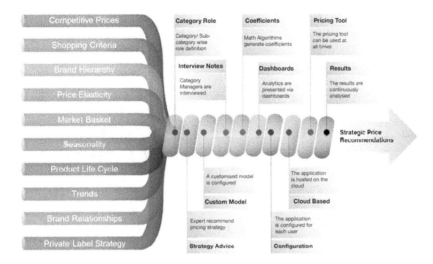

Figure 2.1 Strategic Price Recommendation Framework.

elasticity of demand refers to the ratio of one product's demand when the price of another product changes. While some products are more inelastic by nature such as high-end merchandise or cigarettes, other products can be very elastic, such as milk and eggs. It is also important to note that price elasticity for a product is likely to change by location, time and even by customer.

2.3.1.1 Price Elasticity

The measurement of price elasticity can be quite complex. The impact of the change in demand for a change in price needs to be measured while considering the fact that the demand can change at the same time due to many other factors such as seasonality and competition.

In Figure 2.2, the black bold line indicates the price fluctuation and the bottom shortened lines are promotional events. On 1 April, which is Easter day, the sales rocketed with a drop in price, that is, with a discount. So, initially, customers bought products *en masse*. Later on, the price stayed low, yet the increase in volume did not remain constant for long. Moreover, there was a promotional event again at the end of the month, which resulted in higher sales. This observation spanning over a month depicts price elasticity and the complexity surrounding it.

Price elasticity can be classified into three types which can be observed in Figure 2.3 and it is calculated by dividing the change in demand (or supply) by the change in price.

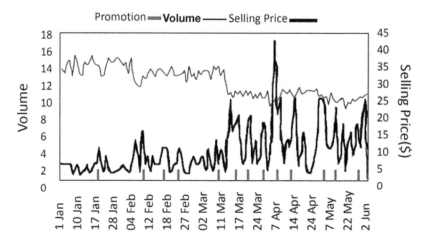

Figure 2.2 Price Fluctuation.

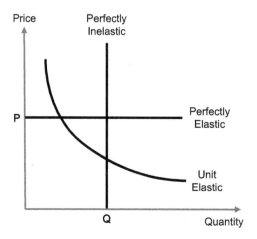

Figure 2.3 Price Elasticity Graph.

2.3.1.2 Elasticity Formula

E = (% change in quantity of X)/(% change in price of Y)

$$E = (\Delta Q_x/Q_x)/(\Delta P_y/P_y)$$

where, Q_x = Quantity of product X, P_y = Price of product Y and Δ = Change

For example, when we change the price of a product from \$10 to \$9 and see an increase in volume from 100 units to 120 units. The calculated Elasticity value is −2.0.

$$E = (\Delta Q_x / Q_x) / (\Delta P_y / P_y)$$
$$\Delta Q_x = Q_2 - Q_1$$
$$\Delta Q_x = 120 - 100 = 20$$
$$\Delta P_y = P_2 - P_1$$
$$\Delta P_y = \$9 - \$10 = -\$1$$

$$E = (\Delta Q_x / Q_x) / (\Delta P_y / P_y)$$
$$E = (20/100)/(-\$1/\$10)$$
$$E = 0.2/-0.1$$
$$E = -2.0$$

In other words, when we reduce the price by 10%, the volume increases by 20% implying an Elasticity value of −2.0.

In technical terms, an item is considered inelastic when the elasticity value is higher than −1, unit elastic when it is equal to −1 and elastic when it is lesser than −1. However, in terms of practical considerations, the below interpretation is more useful.

An Elasticity Value higher than −1.5 indicates that the product is inelastic, and price changes result in a smaller change in demand for the product. Typically these include products where customers have a higher product loyalty or do not care about the price much.

An Elasticity Value lower than −1.5 indicates that the product is elastic, and price changes result in a bigger change in demand for the product. Highly elastic products generally form the "image items" for a retailer. Some Elastic products might have a value as low as −4.0 or −5.0, any value lower than −5.0 needs to be examined closely for potential modelling errors.

In rare cases, certain products demonstrate positive elasticity. This means that an increase in price actually results in increased demand for the product. This is more likely observed in luxury products such as a high-end bottle of wine or perfume, where the customer associates the higher price with a higher perceived quality.

2.3.1.3 Cross Elasticity

The cross elasticity of demand is an economic concept that measures how responsive one product's demand is when the price of another product changes. This measurement, also known as cross-price elasticity of demand, is calculated by dividing the percentage change in the quantity demanded of one product by the percentage change in the price of the other product. In other words, the cross elasticity of demand measures how sensitive a product's demand is to changes in the price of another product.

Retailers use the cross elasticity of demand to set prices for their products. When there is no cross-elasticity of demand to consider, for example, for products with no substitutes, they can be sold at relatively higher prices. Incremental price changes for products with substitutes, on the other hand, are analysed to determine the appropriate level of demand desired and the associated price of the product. Furthermore, complementary products are strategically priced based on demand cross-elasticity.

2.3.1.4 Cross Elasticity Formula

$$E_{xy} = (\% \text{ change in quantity of X}) / (\% \text{ change in price of Y})$$
$$E_{xy} = (\Delta Q_x / Q_x) / (\Delta P_y / P_y)$$
$$E_{xy} = (\Delta Q_x \Delta P_y) / (P_y Q_x)$$

where, Q_x = Quantity of product X, P_y = Price of product Y and Δ = Change

- Positive Cross Elasticity: A positive cross elasticity of demand indicates that as the price of product B rises, so will the demand for product A. This means that items A and B are suitable products. As a result, if B becomes more expensive, people will gladly switch to A. As an example, consider the price of milk. People may switch to 2% milk if the price of whole milk rises. Similarly, if the price of 2% milk rises, whole milk becomes more popular.
- Negative Cross Elasticity: A negative cross elasticity of demand indicates that as the price of good B rises, demand for good A falls. This implies that A and B are complementary items.

2.3.2 Forecast Variables and Factors

Forecasting the sales with a new price point will need the consideration of many factors. These factors need to be considered when modelling retail sales. Some of these factors are discussed below:

2.3.2.1 Seasonality

In retail, seasonality refers to the change in demand with time. Seasonality can be due to a number of factors and are highly also correlated with the location of the demand. For example, the seasonality of demand for a product might be very different in an urban store vs a suburban store during the Christmas season.

- By Time of the Year: Demand for many products are dependent on the time of the year due to factors such as weather, holiday, budgets and events.
- By Holidays: Certain products are very seasonal to holidays. This change in demand due to holidays can be either positive or negative. For example, while the category or toys could see a high demand during Easter, office supplies might see a slower demand during the Holiday season.
- By the Time of the Month: Sales for many products could increase at the beginning of the month and decrease towards the end of the month. This is especially true in developing economies where retail expenditure is a large component of the monthly salary which usually arrives on the 1st of the month.
- By the Day of the Week: Strong relationship between the demand for certain products can be determined by the day of the week. For example, shoppers in certain geographies might prefer to buy more steak as they head towards the weekend. This relationship strength will also vary with the time of the year, a Friday around a summer weekend might see a stronger increase in demand for steak when compared to a Friday in December.
- By the Time of the Day: The time of the day can be modelled against the volume of sales to determine the shopping preference for each product type. For example, the shoppers in the morning may prefer coffee and the shoppers in the evening may prefer wine.

2.3.2.2 Holidays

Consumers shift their purchasing strategies and businesses shift to seasonal selling tactics from Black Friday to New Year's, resulting in drastic shifts in demand and profitability. Businesses that aren't prepared to keep up with the high demand for promotions and intense competitive rivalry during the holiday season may experience stress.

2.3.2.3 Events

Many events such as sporting events, music concerts or business conferences may impact sales which can be either positive or negative in some cases. It is important to note the impact of the event on retail sales generally is location dependent. Further, In-store retail events are an excellent way to engage customers, create brand evangelists, and generate revenue. As a result, they're increasingly becoming a key component of retailers' marketing strategies.

2.3.2.4 Trends

The demand for any product is changing continuously over time. Measuring this change, which can be either positive or negative, gives us the "Trend". To address the ever-changing needs and aspirations of customers today, retail companies need the help of modern marketing analytics software to understand the trends behind the demand. Once again, the trends for each product change by location, time and customer segment.

2.3.2.5 Product Life Cycle

The life cycle of a product refers to the duration of time from when a product is launched or introduced in the market till when it matures or expires and is taken off the shelf. A product's life cycle is divided into four stages: introduction, growth, maturity, and decline. Management and marketing experts use this concept to determine whether to enhance the promotion, change the pricing, expand into new areas, or change the packaging, among other things. Product life cycle management is the practice of planning strategies to continually support and sustain a product as it moves through its following four stages:

1 **Introduction:** During this phase, often a significant amount of money is spent on advertising. Also, the marketing is aimed at raising customer awareness about the product, such as its uses and benefits.

    Pricing New Products: Pricing is an important factor that businesses must consider when introducing a new product or service to the market. Before determining the price of a new product, organisations must understand and calculate the total costs involved in the entire product development process, whether it is designing, manufacturing, or delivering the product. Because no organisation works for free, the price of a new product or service should take into account all of these factors.

2 **Growth:** If the product is a success, it moves on to the next stage, which is growth. Products being introduced into the market might need "investment" which could be done through either offering a lower price or by promoting them to newer customer bases. This is especially important for products with a higher margin or for products which are showing a higher growth rate in other markets.

3 **Maturity:** This is the most profitable stage as production and marketing expenses decrease and the sales reach a healthy plateau. Working with mature products might mean allocating the products a consistent shelf allocation so regular customers can find them at the same location and most likely at the same established price. Often these products do not need an overall promotion but can be introduced to new customers through individual coupons and offers.

4 **Decline:** As other companies try to replicate a popular product's success, the product now faces increased competition, sometimes in the form of improvements or cheaper pricing. The product may lose market share and begin to see a decline in sales.

Dogs/End of Life: End of Life (EOL) refers to when a product has reached the end of its product life cycle and thus can be removed from the assortment. It can be completely removed from the market without replacement or, in many cases, replaced with a new edition. This could be due to a shift in market demand, technology, competitive pressure, and unprofitability, or the product has become obsolete and has been replaced by more functionally advanced technology. When a product becomes obsolete, it is no longer sold, improved, maintained, or supported.

2.3.3 Customer Behaviour

Customer purchasing behaviour is dependent on many aspects of the retail store and not just its price. While there are many factors that can affect the actual visit to a store, there are other factors which determine which product a customer will actually pick up from the shelf for purchase.

2.3.3.1 Market Basket

In retailing terms, a market basket can refer to the constituents of the goods purchased in a single trip or purchase. By analysing the sales data of a retailer at a transaction level (also known as T-Log Data), retailers can make many rich inferences to help them with many merchandising actions. Some of the insights that can be recognised in a market basket analysis include:

- What items are the "Trip Drivers".
- What is the average size of each transaction?
- What items have correlated sales?
- How are transactions sizes different by various seasonality factors.

Products in a Market Basket can be categorised into several categories based on the role they play for the customer.

- Traffic Drivers: There are several perspectives on traffic drivers, and each retailer will approach these products differently. Simply put, these products capture the market's attention and drive them to the store. These could be new products with features that customers haven't seen before, necessary items that the customer might need on a regular basis or items that are only available at the store. Low-cost, well-known, or advertised products may also drive traffic to the stores. These items necessitate a unique set of pricing rules and policies because a customer who is already in the store is likely to buy many other products. That doesn't always mean they have to be the cheapest on the market. Of course, if retailers want to generate traffic at a low cost, your traffic generators must be priced accordingly.

However, if retailers sell one-of-a-kind merchandise or provide features or services (such as training users on how to use new features on their television), retailers may opt for a more expensive traffic generation strategy.

- Basket Builders: Basket builders are products that keep retailers afloat. When customers come to a grocery store they may focus on household staples that families require every week or two. Businesses require traffic generator products to attract customers, but they also require basket builders to generate cross-sell profits. These items should be priced separately from traffic generators. These items may be sold at higher or lower margins depending on the type of merchandise being sold as well as market forces. Creating a secondary pricing strategy for these items can help boost sales and basket profitability.

- Image Drivers: While it is important to be competitively priced, the low margins and frequent price wars or competitive price-comping can drive a retailer out of business with little or no margins. Retailers can have a more intelligent competitive pricing strategy by having lower prices on "Image Items" or "Image Drivers". Image Items can be defined based on elasticity, volume, their role in the market basket and the importance of the item for their customers.

2.3.3.2 Substitute Products

When a customer walks into a retail store to fulfil a particular need, the customer often has several choices to pick from. The products which form the set of products which can serve the customer's need are the substitutable set of products. Substitutable products usually cannibalise the sales of each other. The eventual decision to pick a product will depend on many factors such as the price difference, brand image, packaging and perhaps the location of the product with respect to the customer's line of sight. It is important to understand this set of substitutable products as they can become a component of the price modelling process. Retailers use a concept known as decision-trees to find substitutable products in their assortment.

2.3.3.3 Complementary Products

Complementary products are often connected to each other and do not cannibalise the sales of each other. For example, a customer who is buying a bag of chips might find a dipping sauce to be a complementary product. Retailers can use several analysis techniques, including Market Basket Analysis to understand the complementary nature of products. This could enable the retailers with the right assortment, shelf planning and promotions strategy to increase overall sales and profitability.

2.3.4 Optimal Price

The optimum price is the price at which a retailer's overall profit is maximised. When a price is set too low, the seller sells a large number of units, yet does not make the highest potential profit. When a price is set excessively high, the seller sells too few units, though at a high margin per unit, again resulting in a lower overall profit. By modelling retail sales data, we could determine the elasticity of a product, which could then be used along with the other forecast variables to find the optimal price at which the profit can be maximised.

In Figure 2.4, we note the relationship between volume and price as depicted by the two charts at the bottom of the figure. Each price point has a particular volume of sales associated with this and this relationship is governed by the Elasticity value of the product. The two graphs at the top depict the corresponding profit for each price point. We can note the profit line is an inverted curve meaning with the peak of the curve (maximum profit) is associated with one particular price or the optimal price.

Further, in this example of real sales data from a retailer, we note that reducing the price from $5.99 to the optimal price of $5.49 increases the profit from $234.7 to $244.2. An 8.3% drop in price in this instance is resulting in a profit increase of 4%.

2.3.5 Product Relationships

Product relationships define how different products interact with one another. There are several types of relationships between products that need to be recognised and notated so that the analytical models and the pricing processes can be built in accordance with these relationships. Some examples of the product relationships are discussed below.

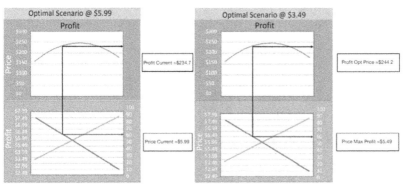

Reducing the price from $5.99 to the optimal price of $5.49 increases the profit from $234.7 to $244.2

Figure 2.4 Optimal Pricing.

2.3.5.1 Line Pricing

Line Pricing is the practice of having the same price for many different products. This is often done to avoid creating confusion in the minds of the consumers and may include a group of products from the same brand for the same size, but have different flavours or variations. (Figure 2.5).

2.3.5.2 Size Relationships

The pricing is based on different sizes of the same product from the same brand. This relationship ensures that the bigger products are priced based on two criteria; larger sizes are priced higher and larger sizes provide better value per unit of measure.

As in Figure 2.6, the product, category and brand are the same but different in size, which introduces different prices. The sugar packet with 2 kg is priced higher than the sugar packet with 1 kg but at a better value per gram of sugar.

2.3.5.3 Brand Relationships

Brand relationships can be used to establish pricing relationships between two brands or to establish pricing relations between a private brand and similar national brand products. Retailers can price private brand products below the national brand to attract traffic and increase sales of the more profitable private label products. A national brand is a product which is owned, designed, manufactured, and marketed by a vendor and distributed across the country under a well-known brand name. National brands, for example, can include Coca-Cola

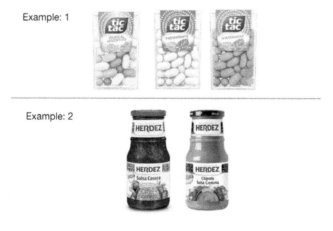

Figure 2.5 Line Pricing.

Figure 2.6 Size Relationship.

and Pepsi, as well as Levi's and Wrangler whereas a private brand, is exclusive to the store and cannot be purchased elsewhere.

National brands typically cost more to promote, and their prices are higher as well. Private-label brands are less well-known and are sometimes regarded as generic or of lower quality. Private label brands, on the other hand, typically have a lower cost basis, allowing retailers to earn higher profit margins.

The retailers typically will sell the private label brands at a lower cost compared to national brands. For private label brands, the retailer could manufacture the products from a third-party (whose factories have excess units to be sold) under the retailer's own brand name. The retailer could have complete control over the product or products. This includes the product's specifications, packaging, and pricing. Private labelling is ideal for retailers and brands with established audiences.

In Figure 2.7, the vegetable salad and sea salt potato chips with the same size and same name are sold under the national brand and private label brand but the price will differ.

2.3.5.4 Brand Hierarchy

Brand hierarchy or brand architecture refers to the structuring of products or services within a brand or company. It refers to the structuring and positioning of

Example: 1

(National Label)   (Private Label)

Example: 2

(National Label)   (Private Label)

Figure 2.7 Brand Relationship.

different products and sub-products and how they relate or differentiate from one another. Every retailer need not create a comprehensive product or service structure. However, retailers who have numerous goods or services in their portfolio, need to structure them to ensure they can determine the best pricing and merchandising strategy for each brand segment.

Some examples of the brand hierarchy are as follows:

- **Good-Better-Best:** Retailers can classify different brands within the same group of products based on the perceived product quality levels. This for example, can be a "Good" brand, a "Better" brand and the "Best" brand. Having this kind of a hierarchical classification will help retailers define pricing strategies that are profitable and clear for the customer.
- **National–Private:** National brands are well-known and trusted by many people because their operations are well-known and they have a high level of accountability. A retailer can define the difference in pricing between these two groups to help drive their private label objectives. It is important to note that in some cases, people might prefer a private brand over a comparative national brand as well.
- **Generic-Branded:** The term generic brand refers to a type of consumer product on the market that lacks a well-known name or logo due to infrequent advertising. Because of the lack of promotion that can inflate the cost of a good or service, generic brands are typically less expensive than their

brand-name counterparts. These brands, which are intended to be substituted for more expensive brand-name goods, are especially prevalent in the food and pharmaceutical industries and are more popular during a recession.

- **Imported–Domestic:** An import is a product in one country but manufactured in another. In many cases, the imported products might be considered as having a higher quality. In other cases, customers might have a higher preference for domestic or local products.
- **Established–New Entrants:** Established products are those that have products that are consistent in design and function, are safe to use and have few defects. Brands that want to enter your market are known as new entrants.

2.3.6 Pricing Rules

While an algorithm or optimisation system can be deployed to determine a price point for maximum profit, it is important to train the algorithm and optimisation system on the various business rules and constraints that need to be considered before determining a final price recommendation.

Various pricing rules are used to define the rules and constraints for the process.

- **Pre-pricing:** Some products in retail come with a fixed price that is usually set by the brand, manufacturer or the government and cannot be changed by the retailer. An example of this could be a postal stamp or an Apple iPhone. It is worthwhile to note that this is different from the concept of MSRP (Manufacturer's Suggested Retail Price) or the MRP (Maximum Retail Price) which usually dictates the maximum price for a product.
- **Ending Digits:** Retailers use the last digits of a product's price to signify how much it has been reduced and whether it can be discounted further. For example, prices with a 4 as the ending, such as $12.94, are for final clearance and will not be reduced further.
- **Brand/Vendor Rules:** One of the key factors for the success of any retailer is to have a strong vendor relationship that can ensure a stable supply, high quality, and lower costs that will ensure profitable operations for the retailer. Analytics can be leveraged to negotiate for lower costs on fewer key items while allowing the vendor to make reasonable margins in other products. In many cases, certain vendor agreements such as to be able to achieve a certain market share for a brand or to maintain price gaps between other competing brands can be addressed as constraints in the pricing process.

2.4 Pricing Process

A pricing process determines how a retailer determines the prices for their products. While pricing is the amount retailers charge for products, product

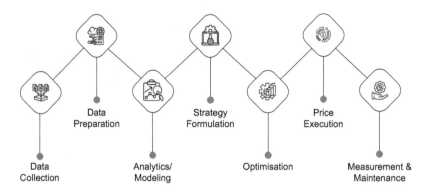

Figure 2.8 Pricing Process.

pricing strategy is how retailers determine that amount. While there are many approaches to the pricing process, one systematic approach to pricing is shown in Figure 2.8.

2.4.1 Data Collection

Data collection is the act of obtaining and evaluating the information on variables of interest in a systematic manner to answer research questions, test hypotheses, make strategic decisions, price products and assess outcomes. (Figure 2.9).

The data for pricing is sourced from the retailers' organisations and external sources. These could be as follows:

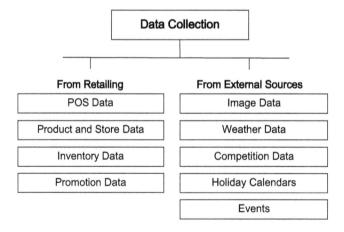

Figure 2.9 Data Collection Sources.

2.4.1.1 From Retailing

- **POS Data:** The data is gathered by the point of sales (POS) system. This includes sales data from the cashier transactions, based on the time of sale, goods purchased, quantity, geographical location and the selling price.
- **Product and Store Data:** All information about a product and the store where it was bought that can be read, quantified, and organised to make it usable is referred to as product and store data. The product data can include additional attributes such as description, brand, size, unit of measure, and other product relationship information.
- **Inventory Data:** The amount of products carried by the retailer by location constitutes the inventory data. This data might need to be segregated based on the amount of products stored at the store, in transit or already ordered.
- **Promotion Data:** Retailers choose to run promotions in different formats based on many factors. Further, this information about the promotions might be stored in various formats and locations based on the need for each category. This might include promotions with regular price discounts or also about promotions through coupons, store placements or advertisements on media.

2.4.1.2 From External Sources

- **Image Data:** This refers to data captured by cameras in a store. This data can provide information on the identification of out-of-stock products on shelves, store traffic, product freshness, store/shelf location and demographics of its customers. These images may help retailers with product recommendations, analysis of future requirements, understanding of region-wise product sales and customer experience recognition.
- **Weather Data:** Weather plays an important role in determining the demand for products. This is because the weather influences consumer purchasing behaviour on a daily basis and it never stops changing; no other external variable shifts demand trends as quickly, frequently, and significantly as the weather. Data from weather can be aggregated at a postal code (or Zip code) level for most countries and connected to the sales of retail by location.
- **Competition Data:** Retailers often already have competitive price information. This data might also be collected from third parties for further analysis.
- **Holiday Calendars:** Holiday dates provide excellent opportunities for retail stores to run effective marketing campaigns and increase sales. This is the most profitable time of year, and every store makes every effort to attract customers and increase sales as much as possible. Information on the holidays can be compiled by the geography of the retailer's operations.
- **Events:** Event information by store location can be prepared for further analysis. It can be useful to both collect historical data and have a mechanism to track events for future events to help with merchandising decisions.

2.4.2 Data Preparation

The process of cleaning and converting raw data before processing and analysing is known as data preparation. This crucial stage before processing includes reformatting data, identifying data errors, and merging data sets to enrich the information.

The process of correcting or eliminating inaccurate, corrupted, poorly formatted, duplicate, or incomplete data from a dataset is known as data cleaning. These issues often occur while integrating data from different sources.

- Errors: For effective analysis, data must frequently be manually transformed or manipulated. When different tables or datasets use different formats for the same information, there is potential for many data errors to become a part of the data set that needs to be rectified before usage.
- Missing Data: In the real world, most datasets have missing data. Before one can use data with missing data fields for analysis and modelling, one must first transform those fields. Understanding the data and the domain from which it originates is critical. Missing values in data is not always a bad thing. Nonetheless, it is an opportunity to perform proper feature engineering to guide the model in interpreting the missing information correctly. There are machine learning algorithms and packages that can detect and deal with missing data automatically. However, it is still recommended to manually transform the missing data using an analysis and coding strategy.
- Duplicates: Data often might be transmitted with duplicate information. Some of the causes of duplicate data include data aggregation and human typing errors. Customers may also provide different information to a company at different times. Data engineering teams will have processes to remove the duplicates before use.
- Incomplete Data: Incomplete data consists of unanswered questions or variables with no observations. For example certain analysis might need 2 years of data or in some cases data from new products or stores might be missing.
- Data Transfer Process: The process of copying data from one location to another is known as data transfer. The data transferred may be transformed in transit or arrive at its destination unaltered. A data transfer consists of at least two steps. The extraction process begins with data extraction from the original source. The data is then written to the destination, a process known as loading. These steps can be carried out either manually or automatically.
- Connecting Different Data Tables: Retailers have data coming from different sources that need to be connected before use in an analytical process. For example, POS data at the transaction level might need to be connected to weather data at the daily level by location or inventory data at the weekly level.
- Modelling Preparation: Several intermediary steps have to be taken on the data set to prepare it for the modelling process.

2.4.3 Analytics and Modelling

Retail data analytics is the process of gathering and analysing retail data (such as sales, inventory, pricing, and so on) in order to identify trends, forecast outcomes, and make better, more profitable business decisions. When done correctly, data analytics enables retailers to gain greater insight into the performance of their stores, products, customers, and vendors — and use that insight to increase profits. (Figure 2.10).

- Historical Sales Analysis
  Analysing sales data is an essential part of retailing. This analysis can help retailers improve its sales, margin and customer satisfaction. Many factors will influence how retailers set up the sales analysis system, including internal sales structure, product, and resources. Whatever the specifics are, there are a few general steps to effectively analysing sales data:

  - Define your goals and metrics.
  - Set up a reporting system.
  - Recognise actionable insights.

- Analytics for Pricing
  Pricing analytics in the retail industry enables businesses to set optimised pricing for specific products, seasons, and stores by analysing lost sales, inventory turn, selling patterns, and other factors.

Category Role Definition: Each category can have a defined role within the overall assortment. For example categories may play one or more of the following roles: bring in new customers, generate traffic, meet the customer's routine needs or serve as a destination for seasonal or occasional purchases.

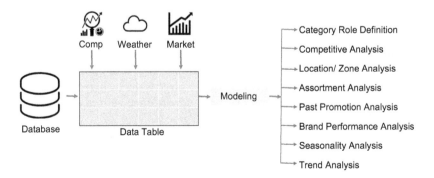

Figure 2.10 Pricing Analytics.

Competitive Analysis: In strategic retail management, competitive analysis is an assessment of the strengths and weaknesses of current and potential competitors. This analysis provides a strategic context for both offensive and defensive opportunities and threats.

Location/Zone Analytics: It is the process of gaining insights from the geographical component of business data. This information for example can be used to establish pricing zones for a retail organisation.

Assortment Analytics: Assortment analysis gives retailers an understanding of how their products are performing based on their attributes and features. This can be used to make merchandising decisions such as floor space, and shelf space, to add products or to discontinue products.

Past Promotion Analysis: This analysis includes the identification of the best-performing campaign types after conducting an in-depth analysis of previous trade promotions. This understanding enables retailers to better allocate future trade promotion investments.

Brand Performance Analysis: The process of measuring the performance of the various brands over dimensions of time, geography or customer segments can constitute a brand performance analysis. Companies can determine their brand's strengths and weaknesses by tracking key performance indicators such as impressions, traffic, and engagement and comparing them to their brand performance goals.

Seasonality Analysis: Seasonality in retail refers to year-round fluctuations in purchasing patterns. The extent to which it affects a store varies depends on the product type and location.

Trend Analysis: Trend analysis is a technique for examining and forecasting the movements of an item using current and historical data.

2.4.3.1 Modelling

Modelling techniques refer to the methods for determining the explanatory variables and coefficients for the demand of a product over time. These variables can include price, seasons and trends. The models are generally built at a product-store level and use several advanced mathematical techniques to understand the complex and intertwined relationships amongst the various factors that affect retail sales.

The process of modelling for retail pricing includes several complex mathematical operations that in many cases are well-evolved and remain the intellectual property of the entities that have evolved and developed these methodologies.

One such modelling process is shown in Figure 2.11.

Some of the common challenges that are associated with modelling include:

- Interpreting the various sales signals that are concurrent in nature, such as seasonality and price changes. The model needs to interpret how much of the impact on sales came from which sales signal.

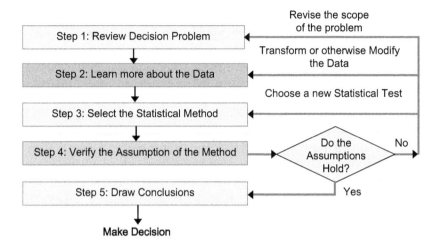

Figure 2.11 Modelling Technique.

- Working with sparse data.
- Borrowing information from similar products or store locations.
- Working with new products or store locations that have no historical data.
- Working with data anomalies such as the Covid-19 situation or a catastrophic weather event.

There are many options for retailers to leverage the models and methodologies that are available in the marketplace. Some of these options include:

- Getting a license to a Do-It-Yourself modelling tool.
- Hiring a company that specialises in retail pricing.
- Hiring qualified resources that are willing to freelance to build models.
- Hiring full-time employees who are qualified and experienced with retail modelling.
- Leveraging coefficients that are industry standards by product and markets.

2.4.3.2 Working with Sparse Data

Data can often be sparse due to many reasons in statistical and computational. There are many challenges in working with sparse data, one of these could be outlier elasticity value (Outliers are values that deviate significantly from the overall pattern of values in a dataset or graph) because of no price change in historical data. In such high dimensional statistics, the data are considered to be sparse when enough sales data are not available. Sparse data is a variable in data analysis in which the cells do not contain actual data. Sparse data is either empty or has a value of zero. It frequently occurs when a large number of customers select a small number of options from a large set of options. Product purchases, movie rentals, social media likes, and electoral votes are a few examples. There are several techniques and algorithms that can be used to infer missing values, remove outliers and borrow information based on product and store hierarchies.

2.4.4 Strategy Formulation

A retailer's bottom line is influenced by a variety of factors, including properly priced products that hit the sweet spot of maximising unit sales without sacrificing profit per unit. Understanding the retailer's cost structure and selecting the best pricing strategy are critical steps toward meeting its profit targets. There are numerous pricing strategies, which is why it may be prudent to experiment until we find the strategy that is most effective for the specific needs of the retailer.

2.4.4.1 Category Management

Product-driven retail businesses require competent Category Management. These managers are in charge of a retailer's product categories and manage the price, promotion, assortment, and vendors. For this, they require adequate market and industry knowledge, and a good understanding of the sales, procurement, and marketing processes.

A few of the core competencies they need to have are:

- Decide on product assortment and pricing that will boost sales.
- Track the demand for new and existing categories.
- Develop an exit strategy for any product that is not doing well.

Category Role Matrices: Retailers can leverage analysis to develop a category role matrix to identify the roles played by each category.

Figure 2.12 displays the category role matrix. The two dimensions used in this example are price sensitivity and volume. Categories here are classified into Profit Drivers, Image Items, Need Visibility and Can be Promoted classification.

Figure 2.13 depicts the role each product plays in each subcategory at a more granular level where the products are again assessed based on elasticity and volume, but at a product level within the subcategory or category.

2.4.4.1.1 PRE OPTIMISATION PREPARATION

Several processes and steps must be taken before a category can be sent to optimisation. Some of these steps are discussed below.

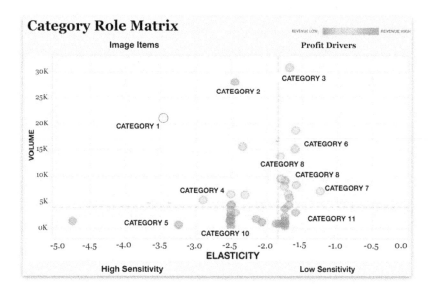

Figure 2.12 Category Role Matrix.

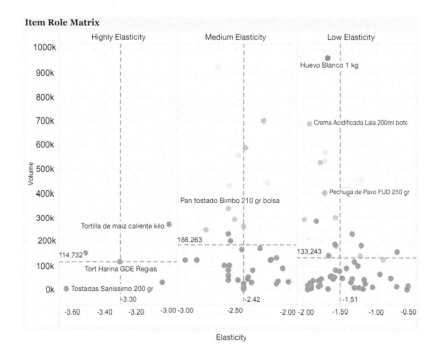

Figure 2.13 Elasticity Analysis.

2.4.4.2 Product Relationship Verification

Before a category can be optimised, it is necessary to verify the various product relationships as defined by the line groupings, size relationships and brand relationships. Oftentimes, the category manager or the pricing analysts are best informed with regard to their categories and should be in charge of doing a final verification and approval of these desired product relationships.

2.4.4.3 Selecting Pricing Rules

There are several rules and considerations that must be incorporated into a price optimisation plan. Some examples of these rules include:

- Pre-pricing rules.
- Product Relationship rules.
- Minimum Margin rules.
- Vendor agreement-based rules.
- Competitive Pricing Rules.

2.4.4.4 Price Optimisation Plan

The price optimisation plan consists of the agreed strategic direction from the category management team. This plan should result from detailed discussions based on the analytical findings and should have a strategic direction for price optimisation in the following dimensions:

- The overall goal of the optimisation- are we targeting profit, revenue or competitive position or a combination of these.
- What is the acceptable change in overall price levels?
- What are the approved product relationships?
- What are my goals for the private label brands?
- Do we have any brand-level hierarchies or relationships to be enforced?
- Are there any promotions being planned in the coming months that might impact base pricing?
- What are the maximum acceptable changes in volume at the product level?
- What are the maximum acceptable changes in prices at the product level?
- What is the desired competitive position?
- Are there any particular vendor agreements that need to be adhered to?

2.4.5 Price Optimisation

Once the modelling is complete and the price optimisation plan is in place, a retailer may begin the process of price optimisation. The calculated coefficients and prepared equations from the modelling phase are now deployed to find out the optimal price for each product-store location.

This optimisation process is usually handled by powerful solvers and computers that are hosted in the cloud. Similar to the approaches used for modelling, the process of optimisation might be best handled in one of the following ways by retailers:

- Using a solver that can be purchased by a service provider.
- Hiring a pricing software company to do the calculations.
- Hiring a freelancer or a consultant to handle the optimisations.
- Build the right team and technology infrastructure to handle the optimisations.

The execution of pricing depends on the mathematical modelling and optimisation process as shown in Figure 2.14.

2.4.5.1 Price Optimisation Data Flow

The flow of data from the stage of POS data collection to the point of optimisation is shown in Figure 2.15.

2.4.5.2 Pricing Process in Retail

The process of implementing the prices from optimisation from the point of collecting the data includes several steps as depicted in Figure 2.16. We can note several review checkpoints and meetings to ensure the mathematical operations are in line with the business requirements.

2.4.5.3 Optimisation Goals, Rules and Constraints

An optimisation can be used to find the price point at which a retailer can make the most amount of profit, however, the optimisation will need several business rules and practical constraints and restrictions as noted below.

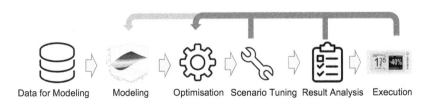

Data for Modeling   Modeling   Optimisation   Scenario Tuning   Result Analysis   Execution

Figure 2.14 Price Optimisation Process.

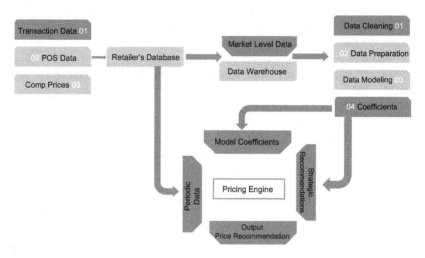

Figure 2.15 Pricing Process Engine.

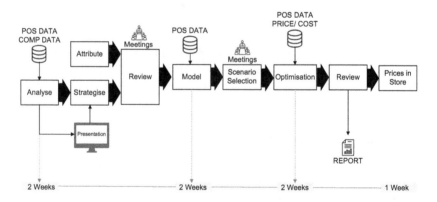

Figure 2.16 Flow Chart for Pricing Model.

2.4.5.3.1 OPTIMISATION GOALS

It is important and necessary to point the optimisation engine towards specific goals surrounding the desired margins, revenue and volume goals.

2.4.5.3.2 OPTIMISATION RULES

The optimisation rules can be used to direct an optimisation towards the business strategy that has been determined. As previously discussed, these rules will include pre-pricing rules, product relationship rules, minimum margin rules, vendor agreement-based rules and competitive pricing rules.

2.4.5.3.3 OPTIMISATION CONSTRAINTS

Many constraints are placed around the volume and price during an optimisation process. Both the Volume and Price constraints may be placed at an item level or for the overall category. For example, we could place a constraint on the optimisation as stated below:

> *"Optimise prices in Category A for maximum profit, while maintaining positive revenue growth without losing more than 1% in overall volume. No product should have a price change or more than 10% and all volume changes at the product level should be less than 20%"*

2.4.5.3.4 GOOD-BETTER-BEST STRATEGY

This refers to a pricing model followed by many organisations that are based on three pricing options for their products using steadily increasing prices. The good version of a product is offered to customers at the market entry level – with the basic, the minimum required features for the buyer. Next, a "better" version of the product with extra features is offered followed by the "best" with many attractive features.

2.4.5.3.5 LAST DIGIT/PRICE ENDING RULES

Mathematical calculations can come back with recommendations not rounded to a complete number or in accordance with what is acceptable as the last digits by a retailer and the retailer's customer. For example, it is simply not common to see a price of $10.37 which may be best rounded off to $10.50 or even better reduced to $9.95.

Retailers should have price digit ending rules that can differ by the range of prices. An example of allowed price endings by price point is shown below:

- For products priced below $10: Allowed ending are .25, .50, .75, .95
- For products priced between $10 and $50: Allowed ending are .50, .95
- For products priced above $50: Allowed endings are .00

2.4.5.3.6 SCENARIO SELECTIONS

The goals and constraints of the optimisation might be tweaked to arrive at various pricing scenarios. The scenarios are likely to be different based on margin, competitive position, price change per cent and other metrics.

Category managers go through a selection process of scenarios based on many considerations.

2.4.5.3.7 TEST AND CONTROL STORES

For in-store product testing or similar experimentation, a set of stores can be classified as Test or Control stores on the basis of their selling pattern, revenue, product assortment, elasticities, location, and demographics, among others.

Once these sets of stores are determined, the price changes (or promotions) are executed in the Test group of stores and its performance is measured against the control stores. This provides an efficient low-risk environment to make better large-scale decisions for the retailers. (Figure 2.17).

2.4.6 Price Execution

The calculated optimal prices now need to be implemented effectively in stores and corrections are made on a timely basis to ensure the prices are working as desired.

- Price Implementation Plan: Important factors to consider in a price implementation plan are:
  - An annual rollout plan that includes all categories and stores.
  - How does the pricing plan interact with the promotions plan.
  - What processes are in place to make corrections to the prices on an ongoing basis.
- Go-Live/Logistics Plan: Retailer often needs to schedule store labour and other technology updates around a Go-Live date. Other important considerations include.
  - Test vs Control stores.
  - Labour allocation and coordination with POS systems.

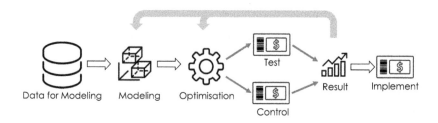

Figure 2.17 Test and Control Stores.

- Price Compliance Verification: Retailers can verify compliance with the new prices both through the POS data and in-store auditing. In many cases, it is possible for a product to display a different price on the shelf and register a different price during the scan/checkout process. This needs to be avoided through processes built for verification and correction of incorrect prices.

2.4.7 Measurement and Maintenance

The saying goes "What cannot be measured cannot be managed". This is especially true in an analytics-driven process where intuition might not be able to give a good read on whether a pricing strategy is working or not.

While measuring profit, revenue and unit sales is most important. Other measures such as measuring the market basket performance, inventory turns, and percentage of a category sales to overall company sales might be good measures as well.

Some of the best practices in Results Measurement include:

- Measuring the performance of the key metrics using various aggregation levels (or filters) such as zones, product groups, category roles or time dimensions.
- Measuring performance as compared to the same periods in the previous years or previous months.
- Measuring performance in Test vs Control Stores.

2.4.7.1 Sales Decomposition Analysis

The sales of a product depends on various factors such as seasonality, trends, base price changes and promotions. Various analytical techniques such as the Sales Decomposition Analysis to extract the impact of price changes after accounting for the component of sales from the other remaining factors (Figure 2.18).

These results are checked continuously such as if the result of a price change is healthy and to confirm no further analysis is required. When the results are found to be unhealthy, re-pricing of the product can be carried out.

2.4.7.2 Price Trackers

The retailer can deploy automated price trackers to monitor the retail prices. A price tracker can search a website for product titles, prices, and availability. Some price trackers go even further, sifting through product descriptions, reviews, pictures, and other pertinent data. Secondly, a price tracker will save the data gathered in a database. A price tracker's user can view this data on a dashboard or in a list style, similar to Excel but generally more sophisticated. A price tracker can be used to monitor the retailer's own prices (this can be done both for brick-and-mortar stores by monitoring the POS systems or for the online store) or to monitor a competitor's prices (online store only).

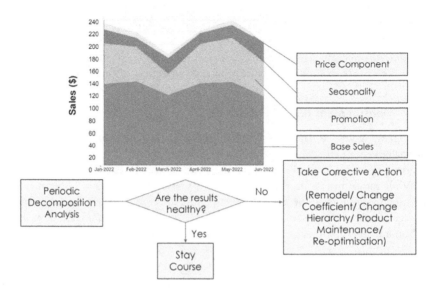

Figure 2.18 Sales Decomposition Analysis Process.

2.4.7.3 Course Corrections

Retailers need to correct or update prices on a continuous basis for many reasons. Some of these reasons are cost changes, competitive price changes or modelling errors.

A modelling or coefficient error can be detected when the actual performance of a product is significantly different when compared to its predicted performance.

2.4.7.4 Weekly Data Monitoring

Retailers can review the purchase and invoice price variations using reports provided by the purchasing department. The Purchase Price Variation Report should ideally be made available weekly to check the accuracy of the standard costs and purchase price variance. This report can also give an insight into buyer behaviour. However, note that any market price fluctuations beyond the control of the buyers and variations in the standard expenses need to be factored into the observations.

2.4.7.5 Monitoring for Price Changes

Price fluctuations and other economic indicators can be analysed to comprehend both the current business scenario and future trends. Price changes can be early indicators of economic change in a region. Here are a few ways in which retailers can monitor pricing data.

- Product Monitoring: Track the prices of the competitor's goods or services in specific retail outlets or regions.
- Global Consistency: Track companies' pricing and promotional initiatives to see if these are consistent in all stores around the world.
- MSRP Benchmarks: Price strategising companies can help develop price trackers and establish benchmarks in a subset of stores regularly, thereby helping in price compliance analysis.
- Monitoring Economic Stressors: Retailers can use Premise data to track price factors in specific places that can serve as early warning signs of economic stress.
- Monitoring Inflation: Track prices of items and commodities for signs of inflation. Or, track changes in inflation within certain regions.
- Pricing Indexes: High-quality and cost-effective pricing indexes can be used to evaluate price changes over time by using fewer observations but achieving the same results.

2.4.7.6 Monitoring for Competitive Price Changes

It is as critical to watch competitors as to watch one's own business. Retailers need to establish the criteria to evaluate the competitor's marketing strategies, customer connection, social media presence, and customer profile, among others. This helps a retailer determine what needs to be done to improve internal processes, earn higher revenues, and ensure customer satisfaction. A detailed discussion on Competitive Prices is handled in Chapter 5.

2.4.8 Evolving the Company Strategy

While a pricing strategy based on analytics is a good starting point and guideline for the initial price optimisation exercise, leveraging the results of the first price implementation can help evolve the overall company strategy effectively.

Based on the results of the prices implemented retailers may realise:

- The earlier assumption on the competition can be more accurate.
- The roles played by each category might have to be updated or this might have changed over time.
- The new products and stores in the retail mix will need to become part of the overall strategy.
- New competitors might have started playing a bigger role or the older competitors might have become weaker.

2.4.9 Assortment-Wide and Store-Wide Rollout Plan

Retailers need to carefully manage rolling waves of optimisation cycles to make sure the available resources are used wisely to have the most profitable prices on their products on a continuous basis. Many factors need to be considered while planning the Rollout Plan.

- Number of products or categories that can be handled by the human and technology resources available.
- Category health deterioration rates. The health of a category, from a pricing perspective, changes over time as new cost changes, new products and new market factors play a larger role over time.

2.4.10 Roles and Responsibilities

2.4.10.1 Human Resources

An organisation's best resource is its workforce. Retail management needs to have the right resources available and be motivated to achieve success in the marketplace. One of the biggest challenges in hiring talented employees in the mathematical and technology fields is the lack of innovation despite routine operations.

For highly skilled and innovative tasks such as modelling or algorithm development, it might be a better idea for retailers to employ third-party resources or even freelancers to address the need. Since these requirements are usually needed for a short period of time and generally need very expensive resources, not having these resources on a full-time basis might be a good idea to consider.

2.4.11 Key Performance Indicators (KPIs)

Key performance indicators (KPIs) may be described as areas to which businesses should pay the greatest attention and on which they can make choices. KPIs, in particular, aid in determining a company's strategic, financial, and operational achievements, particularly when compared to those of other businesses in the same industry. KPIs help retailers see where they are in terms of sales, inventory movement, growth, customer satisfaction, and so on, depending on what they are measuring. Performance indicators can have an indirect influence on company results (for example, measuring employee happiness cannot provide accurate information about whether it improved or worsened business performance, etc.).

Measuring key performance indicators (KPIs) refers to the process of capturing data using specific tools and translating it into meaningful metrics that can be tracked and published in easily digestible charts and dashboards. Most businesses track and evaluate operational data. These indicators can then be used to improve operational efficiency.

KPI tracking helps fine-tune and correctly orient businesses for success. Creating a suitable KPI collection is the first step toward successfully monitoring an organisation's performance indicators. The performance of various areas of a business can be measured, analysed, and improved by measuring the relevant KPIs. Especially, sales, where monthly sales and generated leads can be quantified and tracked.

KPI tracking activities when tied to sales activities can boost a store's success. Regular monitoring of these predictive metrics allows shop managers to forecast future sales and spot patterns. This data helps retail managers better evaluate customer behaviour. This data can also be used for knowledge sharing among all divisions within an organisation, such as marketing, and visual merchandising, among others. Following are some of the important sales KPIs that need to be tracked and the benefits they offer.

1 Departmental or Category Sales: For businesses that sell a wide range of products, a data dashboard displaying a comparative category-wise sales volume of all the products is a useful management information tool. This information can help the merchandising department strategically structure product shelving and advertising. For example, a manager of a sportswear store can prominently display the soles of sneakers, especially if these account for the majority of global sales. Merchandising decision-makers will be able to reorganise space to display these items near the store's entry. This can result in a high conversion rate and enhance customer satisfaction.

2 Average Purchase Price: This sales KPI measures the average value of each purchase made by customers and compares that with the average number of units per transaction. This metric helps assess purchasing trends of customers. and can help boost overall sales. This data can also be collected using data storytelling software. It can also help in customer classification based on demographic features, among others.

3 Assessing Sales Volume: This KPI helps assess the effectiveness of advertising activities, track and monitor consumer spending habits, analysing promotions, among others.

4 Turnover of Inventory: The inventory turnover ratio refers to the number of times the inventory has been sold and replaced over a specific time period. A high turnover ratio indicates that the business is doing well. If the turnover ratio is poor, it could mean that the sale is low or the supply is in excess. In this case, the retailer needs to look at the supply chain process for bottlenecks. This KPI data is critical for retail managers and decision-makers to assess which items to focus on.

5 Gross Margin Return on Investment (GMROI): GMROI is another important KPI to analyse. It allows retailers to see how much money the

firm has recovered for each dollar invested in inventories. Tracking this critical performance metric provides a more realistic assessment of inventory planning. This is the most appropriate method for making better selections regarding which products to keep and which to discard.

6   Product Demand: Which products sell fast? Which products are most profitable? Tracking product performance KPIs can provide the answers to these questions. This metric is based on goods sold over a certain time period using an inventory of the best-selling items for a specific time period: a week, month, or year. Knowing which products perform best and worst helps the store manager decide which are worth investing in and which should not be reordered. They can anticipate customer demand and thereby increase sales and ensure customer satisfaction.

7   Foot Traffic or Footfall: The number of people who enter a store is referred to as foot traffic. This can be measured by customer counters and retail sales analysis. Tracking this parameter over time indicates hours or seasons when more or less staff assistance is required, apart from assisting in-store management. Foot traffic helps marketing teams assess a campaign's success. Merchandisers can also assess the success of their window displays using this information.

8   Conversion Rate: The conversion rate is the percentage of visitors to a retail outlet who make a purchase. It refers to the number of visitors who convert into customers when they make a purchase. This conversion could be a purchase or even registration to a loyalty card. This KPI is critical for retail managers to track and assess their marketing strategy effectiveness. Measuring this data allows retailers to find good practices and expand them to other stores.

9   Customer Retention: The rate at which customers return to the store is referred to as customer retention. This metric helps gauge consumer satisfaction, the breadth of offerings, and the quality of products. By sharing this information with stakeholders, an organisation can develop marketing strategies and promotions at key periods. This KPI can also be used as part of a loyalty programme plan to encourage customers to return to the store.

2.4.12 Vendor Relationships

Vendor relationship management (VRM) is a type of business activity made possible by software tools that aim to give retailers' efficiency in doing business with their vendors. Vendor management enables a retailer to control supply chain expenses, reduce possible vendor risks, ensure efficient service delivery, and get long-term value from suppliers. This involves collating price information, assessing the quality of work, managing communication with suppliers, managing payments, and evaluating performance by establishing organisational standards.

In the past, often confrontational strategies would be used in procurement. Today's strongest vendor relationships are more like partnerships or strategic alliances with cooperation and information sharing as major drivers of mutual success. Thus, vendors, as business partners, play a critical role in an organisation's success or failure. Organisations should try to develop vendor relationships in the same way they work to promote customer loyalty. Having a good working connection with a supplier provides the following benefits.

- Cost Savings: Being a good customer to a vendor with consistent orders and on-time payments can earn the retailer volume discounts and special promotions.
- Deliveries on Time: Retailers need the materials on time to provide good service to their own customers. A good relationship could mean that the vendor will put the retailer first and deliver supplies ahead of schedule! That too is of the best quality.
- Vendor Support: When difficulties emerge such as late or damaged shipments, the vendor will respond quickly. They will efficiently resolve any issues and provide reimbursements.
- Customisation Opportunities: As the vendor gains a better understanding of a retailer's business, they may be able to supply unique and exclusive goods that can provide the retailer with a competitive advantage over competitors.
- Customer Satisfaction: A positive client-vendor connection can have an influence on another relationship: between the customers – the end-users of the business. Customers will appreciate the final product or service, and its quality. This may help build customer loyalty and trust.

Thus, vendor management is critical for business continuity and achieving business objectives.

2.4.12.1 Vendor Management Process

The vendor management process involves a series of tasks, which are as follows.

- Vendor Selection: The first step in the vendor selection process comprises researching and obtaining quotations from prospective vendors and then obtaining quotations via requests for quotation (RFQs) and requests for proposals (RFPs). While costing will undoubtedly play a role in the selection process, businesses need to consider other aspects when selecting vendors: vendor's reputation, capacity, track record, and communication channels.
- Contract Negotiation: It is critical to get the contract right from the start and ensure that the conditions agreed upon are beneficial to both parties. Negotiating a contract takes time. It entails specifying the products or services, the start and end dates of the agreement period, and other important

terms and conditions. Confidentiality and non-compete provisions may also require special consideration.

- Vendor Onboarding: This entails obtaining the necessary documents and information to establish the vendor as a company-approved supplier and includes a payment guarantee to the vendor. The onboarding process may also contain information, such as the vendor's appropriate licenses, tax papers, insurance data, and contact details.
- Monitoring Vendor Performance: Retailers need to monitor and assess their vendor's performance as part of the vendor management process. This might involve assessing their performance on KPIs, like product quality and quantity, and delivery dates.
- Risk Monitoring and Management: Vendors should be assessed for posing potential threats to the supply chain and the organisation. This could be compliance violations, litigation, data security concerns, and intellectual property theft. A vendor's conduct or inability to provide products and services on time could disrupt operations.
- Payment Terms: This is critical as it can be a potential flashpoint. Retailers need to ensure that suppliers are paid on time and according to the agreed-upon conditions for the goods and services they deliver.

2.4.13 Leveraging the Pricing Process for Promotions and Markdowns

Several of the data and technology infrastructures can be leveraged for the processes of running promotions and markdowns. The differences are discussed in detail in the upcoming chapters of Promotion and Markdown.

Chapter 3

Promotions

3.1 Introduction

Promotions in retail play a key role in retail business by driving traffic, building the price image, boosting sales volume and increasing profit. When combined with everyday pricing and advertising, promotions can be a powerful mechanism for a retail organisation to leverage for success. Though the process of funding and executing promotions has evolved over the years, the current system is still cumbersome and slow which can be improved through analytics and technology.

3.2 Promotion Strategy Formulation

What a retailer wants to accomplish in terms of promotion is a key factor in developing a promotion strategy. It could be as simple as informing prospective customers about what retailers sell and how the products can benefit the customer.

Formulating an effective promotions strategy can include many components. As a first step a retailer must list out the objectives for running the promotion or what would define the success of a promotion. Once this is done, the retailer can plan for the promotional strategy and the steps involved to achieve it.

3.2.1 Promotion Objectives

The basic objective of promotions in retail is to increase sales, advertise a product or service, and highlight its unique selling proposition. To elaborate:

- Increase Sales: We now know a decrease in price results in increased demand. When this decrease in sales is advertised as a temporary decrease in price, such as through a "sale" sticker, coupon, or a discounted price label, this is known as a promotion. A trained customer eye recognises this as a temporary opportunity to buy at a lower price and oftentimes, the lift in sales seen for a "promoted price" is higher than the lift in sales seen for the same product at the same lower price. This additional lift is called a "promotional lift".

DOI: 10.4324/9781003382140-4

- Advertise a Product: With promotions, consumers can be made aware of the presence of the product in the market and know how it works for them. The right tactic of advertising would be determined based on the audience and the product being promoted. In many cases, promotions can be used to bring attention to new products, products that have a higher margin, and those which are highly elastic.
- Build an Image: Many retailers often aim to build an image of having the best price or of having lower prices in the market. To do so, using promotional tactics on image items − or items that have high elasticity and high volume − can be a very effective tool.

3.2.2 Promotional Strategies

Promotion Strategy

For a winning promotion strategy, a few essential steps that retailers can follow are shown in Figure 3.1.

Let us look at these steps closely:

1 List the Promotional Objectives: Setting goals is crucial to implement a promotion. It provides not just a sense of purpose but keeps the team productive and reach their objectives. Consider what needs to be accomplished

Figure 3.1 Promotion Strategy.

and set the objectives. If retailers set goals they have no control over or make them dependent on others, the progress may be stifled.

Promotions can be:

- Define SMART (Specific, Measurable, Achievable, Realistic and Timely) Objectives.
- Align the goals with the overall marketing strategy.
- Set metrics to measure the results.
- Brainstorm on the call-to-actions to use.

2 Create a Budget and Plan: When it comes to budgeting, it is critical to strike a balance with the objectives. Determine with a plan how much needs to be spent on each campaign to achieve the objective. Even for low-cost, interactive, online, and effective targeting, companies still want to save money.

- Prioritise the objectives and set a budget.
- Plan the promotion to make the best use of the allocated budget based on ROI (Return on Investments).
- Use targeting to get the biggest return from the audience within the desired market.

3 Determine the Target Market: Narrowing down the target market will ensure that time, effort, and money are efficiently used. Learn about the competitor's strategies and research the market well. The Target market can be determined based on geography, demographics, income levels and user personas.

4 List the Types of Promotions: Retailers have a wide array of promotions that can be chosen based on the products and markets being promoted. The type of promotions can be different based on the customer segments being targeted. Moreover, retailers today can consider adopting SEO and developing a location-based online marketing solutions. Finally, retailers can choose the promotion types based on the objectives and budget availability.

5 Develop Marketing Messages: Next step is to create the marketing message for the promotion now that you know the target market and promotion type. The marketing message is a crucial aspect of a promotional campaign. It catches attention, explains how the product relates to the consumers, and encourages them to try it. People will not pay attention to advertisements unless they come with a compelling message. In brief, the message can be based on the following aspects:

- Identify the pain areas of the target market.
- Highlight the values, benefits, and the product's unique selling proposition.
- Keep the message clear and sharp, using keywords the market is familiar with.
- Change the message depending on the market and explain how the product will benefit them.

6 Develop a Promotional Strategy: Developing the promotion plan entails figuring out how the details and a roadmap to meet the promotional

objectives. Identify how to raise awareness, and pique the target audience's interest to convert them into consumers. Every activity needs to generate revenue for the company. The plan has to include timelines for each activity.

7 Execute and Track the Activities: Finally, disseminate information about the promotion. Track the performance of every activity to make quick corrections wherever required. That will make it easier to adapt the strategy and avoid any inadvertent mistakes by catching these early on.

- Review the objectives on a regular basis.
- Ensure that you are monitoring the right metrics.
- Do not make conclusions without sufficient data.
- Be alert and flexible to make minor changes if required.

3.2.3 Types of Promotions

There are many different types of promotions a retailer can leverage. The selection of the right type of promotion for a retailer may depend on many factors such as timing, trade funds, volume goals, labour logistics, and competitive strategies.

Promotions can be classified based on price promotions, coupon promotions and loyalty-based promotions.

1 Price Promotions: A reduced price point is used to promote the sales of a product. This reduction in price has to be temporary in nature, which means the discount has to be removed after a certain time period to go back to the original base price. This discounted price can be conveyed in different forms. A few of these examples are:

- 20% Off.
- Buy 1 Get 1.
- Buy 2 Get 1.
- 50% Off 2nd Item.

   In other variations, promotions may be used as incentives to promote additional products or new products. Some examples of these are:

- Buy goods over $100 to get 20% off.
- Free tote bag with all purchases over $200.
- Free baby shampoo with the purchase of 50 Pack baby diapers.

2 Coupon Promotion: Coupons are a way of targeting value-conscious customers by providing them with a better price individually instead of a discounted price for all customers. Customers who are willing to save and produce coupons for their purchases can enjoy discounted prices while providing valuable information to the retailers on the level of discount that is effective and how it is different for different customer bases.

Coupons can involve clipping a ticket from a newspaper or a periodical and redeeming it at a business. Depending on how the offer is specified, a coupon might be applied to a certain product or an entire transaction. The coupon may only be redeemed once and only by the coupon's owner.

Some of the best practices to be used with couponing include:

- Selecting coupons based on price elasticity.
- Targeting coupons to the right target customer segment.
- Leverage coupons to promote basket size.
- Leverage coupons to promote new products.
- Ensure proper integration with the POS systems.
- Train employees on the Coupon redemption process.
- Have an expiration date.
- Set limits on coupons per customer or transactions.

3 Loyalty-based Promotion: Discounts can be customised to each customer based on the loyalty of the customer to a particular retailer. Often a common methodology to determine this loyalty is based on an RFM analysis which stands for Recency-Frequency-Monetary value of the customer transactions.

The following are examples of typical incentives:

- Prior notification/early access to new items.
- Price discounts on items that are not applicable to other customers.
- Early access to special offers.
- Free merchandise or special service.
- Free or expedited shipping.
- Discounts for privileged customers/members only.

Many regular customers are asked to register with the retailer and provide contact information and sometimes other details after which they are given a unique identification, such as a membership card, to join a loyalty programme, also known as a rewards programme or points programme. When such customers make a purchase, they are given special points for discounts and other offers.

4 Competitive Promotion: A competitive promotion occurs when retailers match the price of another competitor just to ensure the customer will not leave to go to another retailer. There are often limitations around these promotions and do not apply to the prices of online retailers.

3.2.4 Promotion Considerations

When deciding on a promotion, retailers need to consider many factors that are important for the business. While the decision of the right promotional product and its price can be determined through analytics, the overall mechanism for the promotions is a company-wide strategic selection that should be based on important considerations such as the ones listed below. (Figure 3.2).

Figure 3.2 Science of Promotion.

Nature of Product: Different promotional tools are required for different products. For example, personal selling is suitable for industrial items, such as machinery, equipment, and real estate as these require a lot of pre-sale and after-sale services to sell, install, and maintain, among others. Advertising and publicity, on the other hand, are better suited to consumer products, particularly convenience items.

Nature of Market: Promotion is significantly influenced by the quantity and location of customers. Personal selling is effective when the pool of potential consumers is limited and focused on a specific area. However, if the customer base is big and diverse, a combination of advertising, personal selling, and sales promotion is required to sell the goods. The customer type can also have an impact on the promotions. For example, advertising can be significantly different based on geography, education, income and age of the consumer segments.

Stages of a Product's Life: As a product progresses through its life cycle, the nature and intensity of its promotion change. At the introduction stage, the aim of the promotion is to generate primary demand by stressing the product's characteristics, utility, and so on. Therefore, a combination of advertising and publicity is required. As the product matures, promotion and personal selling become important to retain client demand. Finally, during the decline stage, promotional activities are reduced. A greater focus is placed on sales marketing to boost decreasing sales.

Availability of Funds: A promotion is determined by the marketing budget. If the budget is high, many promotional tools can be used. However, if the budget is restricted, which is often the case, companies need to select the tools carefully.

Nature of Techniques: Certain techniques used in promotions have distinct characteristics that make an impact. For example, advertising is an impersonal method of communication that reaches the masses. Outstanding or imaginative styles of presentation and use of colours and music have a lasting image of a brand in the minds of customers. Personal selling entails face-to-face connection with customers. This helps build effective personal relationships. Similarly, a sales promotion is a set of short-term incentives offered to customers to increase sales for a limited time.

Promotional Strategy: A promotion is primarily determined by a company's strategic approach, which can be a push or pull approach. When a manufacturer requires dealers to carry the product and market it to customers, is a push approach. That is, persuade potential consumers to buy it. Personal selling and trade promotions are examples of this push approach. In a pull strategy, customers purchase goods on their own initiative. Advertising and consumer promotion are examples of this pull approach.

Readiness of Buyer: Different promotional materials are required at various levels of buyer preparedness. For example, during the understanding stage, a combination of advertising and personal selling is critical. Whereas, personal selling is more successful in the conviction stage. When it comes to closing sales, a combination of sales advertising and personal selling is effective.

3.2.5 Promotion Channels

To reach their target audiences, businesses can use various channels of promotions alone or in combination. Depending on the products and services offered, each company can target a specific audience. It is important to note the goal of this chapter is to determine the right price and the right channels for retail promotions.

Direct marketing: Direct marketing reaches out to specific companies or individuals to inform them of upcoming sales, services, or new products. E-mails, direct mail, phone calls, and flyers are all examples of direct marketing. Direct marketing is a quick and efficient method of promoting products and services. Companies, for example, can reach out to customers through a targeted e-mail campaign.

Sales promotion: A sales promotion is a short-term initiative that is used to increase product demand and sales. Flash sales, giveaways, coupons, and loyalty reward programmes are all examples of sales promotions. This method of promotion is effective for announcing new products, engaging new customers, and selling out of an old product's remaining inventory. Because of the surge in product demand and the use of competitive pricing, businesses may use sales promotion to maintain popularity during the holiday seasons.

Digital marketing: Content marketing, search engine optimisation, social media marketing, and affiliate marketing are all examples of digital marketing. Companies can connect with a larger audience by using digital marketing. This method of promotion is also very effective because it can operate on a global scale in a short period of time.

Personal selling: Person-to-person communication is part of the personal selling strategy. This could include meeting with customers in person or over the phone. Personal selling aims to build meaningful relationships with customers or clients. Car dealerships are an example of a company that uses personal selling because they rely heavily on developing relationships with their customers in order to gain their trust and loyalty.

General advertising: General advertising is a type of promotion that does not target a specific audience but instead seeks to raise general awareness of a company or product. Businesses use this method to improve brand recognition by utilising mass media advertising such as magazines, billboards, radio, and television. General advertising usually has several goals, such as promoting a product to first-time buyers, establishing a brand in the market, encouraging existing users to purchase new services, and launching new products.

Public relations: Public relations, also known as PR, helps to maintain a company's public image. When a company employs public relations, it hopes to influence how its target audience perceives it. Press releases, publicity stunts, and social media endorsements are all examples of PR campaigns. This strategy can assist a company or brand in protecting, improving, or rebuilding its reputation.

Sponsorship: Sponsorship is a common form of promotional marketing in which a company pays a fee to a person or contributes to the funding of an event in exchange for publicity and advertising. Businesses can increase the credibility of their advertisements by partnering with a well-known person or brand through sponsorships. Having the backing of a powerful person or a well-known brand can boost your popularity, sales, and reputation.

3.3 Science-Based Promotions

While retailers have been running promotions for 100s of years, the process of running a promotion has almost become standardised in the industry. Although there are some variations based on the geography and the type of retail involved, the basic pillars of the promotion mechanism in retail have evolved but unfortunately, the current state does not leverage the full potential of data analysis and the latest technology available to its full potential.

In this chapter, we look at several factors which are key components of the promotional strategy and we also discuss the key considerations of the nuances of customer behaviour and the rules of promotion as applicable to a science-based promotions process.

3.3.1 The Promotional Lift

When the price of a product is reduced for a short duration of time and the corresponding price discount is advertised by a retailer in any form, it is called a Retail Promotion. The additional sales generated by this promotional price are higher than the additional sales by a non-promoted discounted price, even though the discount levels in both cases might be exactly the same. This is due to the fact that the customers behave differently when they see a promoted price change when compared to every price change. This increase in sales when compared to the earlier sales level before the promotion is called the promotional lift (Figure 3.3).

3.3.2 Factors Related to Retail Promotions

3.3.2.1 Cannibalisation Effect

Cannibalisation is the effect of a new or promoted product makes on the sale of related items. When a certain product is promoted, the increased sales for the promoted product might come from cannibalising the sales of the same or another substitute product that might have sold at a regular non-promoted price.

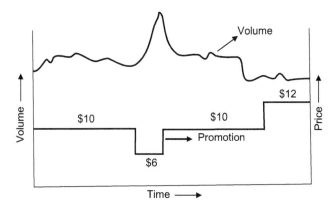

Figure 3.3 Promotional Lift.

3.3.2.2 Pantry Loading

Running a promotion can result in a loss of sales at a later time. This happens as a customer might buy more products than needed at the time of purchase to reduce his cost of purchasing at a later point in time. This is especially true in cases of products that have a higher shelf life and can easily be stored such as paper towels and diapers. While it may still be beneficial for a brand or a manufacturer to lock in future sales from a customer through promoting pantry loading, the retailer often can lose future sales due to the pantry loading effects of current promotions.

3.3.2.3 Trade Funds

Retail promotions can be partly or fully funded by trade funds provided by the brand or manufacturer of the product being promoted. This allows the retailer to lower the cost of running promotions while purchasing and selling more products for a particular brand or manufacturer.

The process of working with trade funds works like a well-oiled machine in many cases and has several interworking processes across multiple organisations. In most companies, marketing administrators and account managers manage finances for promotions. For example, a major beverage manufacturing retailer creates a new fruit-flavoured beverage. The account manager intends to launch a campaign with a new presentation. The manager uses the budget set aside by the marketing administrator for advertising.

3.3.2.4 Promotion Constraints

Marketing can also have limitations in its ability to drive sales. Promotions may not attract the target customers retailers do not get the appropriate price

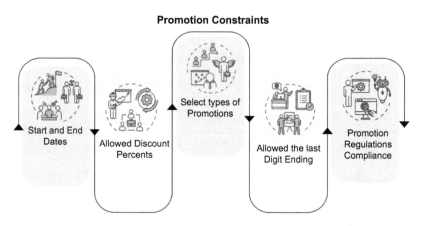

Figure 3.4 Constraints in Retail Promotion.

approach. The market size, existing demand for a product, and competition all play a part in making a promotion successful. Moreover, the retail management's approach and budget also affect the outcome of a promotion. The constraints of promotion are captured visually in Figure 3.4. Let us look at these more closely:

1 Start and End Dates: It is not easy to decide upfront when exactly to start promotion and gauge the time to end it when demand starts falling. Flash sales.
2 Types of Discounts: A discount is a reduction in the price of products or services. It denotes that a product is being sold for a price cheaper than its regular price. Usually, discounts are given in percentages. Sometimes, it is given as a fixed amount of the regular price of goods or services. Discounts can be of different types. Like, a quantity discount is a discount based on the number of goods bought. Then, a trade discount is given by suppliers to distributors. Distributors, in turn often pass on the discount to customers by offering low prices of such products. Then there are promotional discounts, which are a common approach for promoting sales. For example, during a sale, a shirt may have 15% off or if you buy one shirt, you get another one free.
3 Types of Promotions: The purpose of promotions is to get seen and stand out. Select the type of promotion carefully – whether it be in a new market, launching a new product, or warding off competition. Thus, select the promotional activities that will best serve the promotional objectives: be it advertising, personal selling, telemarketing, and publicity through billboards, short or long sales promotions, and direct marketing, among others.
4 Last Digit Endings: The retailer's final promoted price should have the last ending digits in line with the previously defined price ending rules. In some cases, retailers use different last-digit ending rules to identify the promoted price.

5   Regulations and Compliance: Retail promotions are implemented by marketers who may not be aware of the laws and regulations governing marketing and discounts. Retailers often follow pricing methods and procedures that have been in place for a long time. Not realising that certain laws may have changed over time, thereby sometimes running into legal complications. (Discussed further in Section 3.4).

3.3.3 Modelling Retail Promotions

The fundamental evaluation of sales promotions reveals the promotion's impact on sales, revenue, and profitability. It does not, however, provide answers to several critical questions, including those listed below:

Price Discount Levels: The price discount levels profile list assists retailers in setting up and tracking discounts (reductions) and markups (increases) to your standard pricing for the goods and services you sell. There are four price discount levels, which are as follows:

- Company – refers to all products and customers.
- Item – the price level that is assigned to items (e.g volume discounts).
- Customer – Prices that can be assigned to customers.
- Price levels that can be assigned to vendors.

Promotion Flags: Running a promotion in retailers can take different forms and it can be different for each retailer. While some promotions can simply be about reducing a price temporarily with a new price tag, others can mean elaborate display units or premium end-of-aisle locations. Others can include flyers, announcements, or even TV advertisements. From a mathematical perspective, it is important to identify these promotions to be able to measure their impact against the sales volume. This is typically done by assigning "flags" or in most cases using a value of "1" or "0" to identify each promotion data in a time series. When modelled, these flags can provide very valuable insights into the impact of each promotion type which can further help in selecting the most effective promotion types based on the Return on Investment or ROI.

3.4 Promotion Process

When processing retail promotions, retailers look for the most effective communication channels and tactics to reach customers. Retailers will collaborate with the team in merchandising, marketing, finance, supply chain, and promotions to re-engineer the promotional process so that all stakeholders have the right information at the right time, the first time, and the customers have the right items at the right price.

Retailers work to improve promotional effectiveness within the company by implementing standard marketing processes, developing a marketing strategy and calendar, allocating necessary resources, and carrying out the promotion plan. Retailers gather data to determine whether the promotion is ready for the customer and then follow up to ensure that the plan is carried out at the store level. Retailers also improve distribution and product flow by confirming inventory readiness to stores during a promotion. Most importantly, retailers conduct a post-project analysis to identify areas for improvement as well as additional customer insights for future improvement (Figure 3.5).

3.4.1 Promotions Data Infrastructure

The data infrastructure needed for promotions is similar to the data requirements of a base pricing model. However, the promotions modelling process requires information about the various promotion channels that have been deployed in the past and which may be deployed in the future.

Oftentimes, different category managers end up using their own systems and perhaps spreadsheets to track and manage their promotions. This can be challenging to integrate into the overall promotions planning process. Different trade fund management systems that are available in many parts of the world can provide an easy interface to leverage the data from the promotions process with promotion modelling, analytics, and optimisation.

3.4.2 Promotional Products/Market/Duration Identification

Promotional products are items imprinted with a company name, logo, or slogan and distributed for free or at a very low cost in order to market or promote a

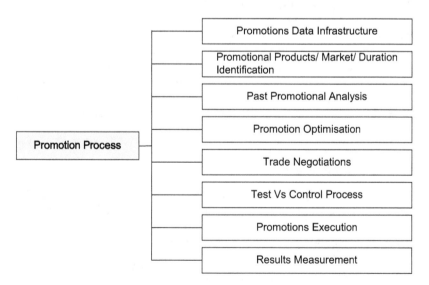

Figure 3.5 Promotion Process.

brand. They are frequently used at trade shows and events, as part of a creative marketing campaign, or as a corporate gift.

A retailer's product selection and stock levels are critical. Nobody can give the customer everything all at once, but the product selection should provide enough alternatives. If a client looking for a dress cannot find one in red, she should be able to choose a blue one instead. Sales success requires offering the right product at the right time and place to the right customer. The right product selection drives not only the energetic growth of large corporations but also the growth of small businesses. By changing and improving product selection, a retailer can increase the number of purchasing customers. Selection corrections help customers find the product they were looking for or a sufficiently similar one that meets their needs. It is therefore recommended to analyse the buyer's critical deciding factors while in the store – product price, brand, size, taste, colour, and so on. It's also a good idea to consider what alternatives customers might have if they can't find the perfect product.

Right Product: Product marketing is no longer a guessing game thanks to tracking and reporting technologies. Buyer interest in specific goods and services can be observed, and their opinions of previously acquired goods can also be ascertained. With such knowledge, retailers can modify the messaging and product marketing plan. It's also critical to understand how the length of the sales cycle varies depending on the product. In this manner, retailers can modify the marketing, focusing on various product-specific pain areas. Retailers are better able to offer the more they comprehend the purchasing motivations of their customers.

Right Place: Not only what retailers say matters, but also where they say it. Just half the battle is won by being aware of a lead's interests and preferences. Retailers must be aware of the preferred methods of contact with clients. They should keep tabs on how leads are responding to their emails, how they are looking up the retailer's company or items online, and which social media platforms they are using to discuss the relative advantages of various goods and services. Even if the message is the best in the world, it will be ignored if retailers deliver it to the incorrect audience.

Right Time: The ideal time is more like a perpetual "now". Leads should be reached when they are considering the retailer. Today, marketers have access to a wide variety of real-time data. Retailers can phone a person while they browse their website or tweet about your offering. Emails can be directed at specific recipients, linking leads to the type of material that encourages them to seal a sale. Additionally, the process can be automated through lead nurturing, ensuring that based on the stage of the buying cycle a lead has reached, specific activities done by the lead will trigger the appropriate content.

3.4.2.1 Product Identification

Products for promotions should be selected based on a number of factors and can be done so using analytics-based strategies for ongoing operations.

Some of the factors for identifying products for promotions can include:

- Taking into consideration the "item role" as defined in strategic analysis.
- Past performance on promotions by the same or similar products.
- Competitive promotions in similar categories/time frames.
- The vendor agreed negotiations and targets previously set for volumes.
- Promoting future "cash cow" or "profit driver" products.

3.4.2.2 Market Identification

Not all products can be promoted similarly across all markets. For example, a gardening tool is best advertised in a suburban store and probably not in a store in the city centre.

Selecting one or more market segments or consumer groups to include in your marketing mix is known as target market identification. Mass marketing to every potential customer in the market as a whole can eventually be less beneficial for the company than customising that mix to match the specific wants and preferences of your target market.

No matter how universally enticing you believe your good or service to be, not everyone will require or choose to purchase it, and especially not everyone will be willing to pay the same price for it. Additionally, it can be costly and time-consuming to focus your marketing efforts on the general market (whether it be the consumer, industrial, or reseller sector). Retailers should consider using a targeted marketing strategy to narrow down their target market from the larger market and concentrate their marketing mix on that market in order to increase their reach and profitability.

The needs of different segments of the market are different based on many factors such as demographics, household size, degree of competition, price elasticity, and convenience of store locations. Analytics should be used to determine which products are a good fit for promotion in which markets. This analysis can be further improved by adding the dimensions of time -when should the promotion be run and also for exactly how long.

3.4.2.3 Promotional Period

A promotion that runs for a set time duration is referred to as a promotional period. Retailers define a promotion's sales period, purchasing period, listing window, and the last date for a good receipt in stores. With this information, retailers can establish the exact day on which promotional products need to reach the distribution centre to be delivered to the retailers on time. For example, when sourcing promotional merchandise, a distribution centre may send sale products to a location two days before the start of a campaign, but to another destination a week before the start of the offer.

Also, listing regulations denote which store can sell or reorder articles and when. The promotional system will generate a warning alert if a store regularly sells winter gloves only until the end of March. Retailers can design a promotion that extends into April. However, retailers can override the notice to allow the store to offer winter gloves in April.

Each retailer or store making an offer can have different validity period dates. For example, a swimwear promotion may begin earlier and stay longer in stores located in warmer areas than in those located in colder areas. If separate promotional periods are defined for distinct store groups, the overall promotion period is defined as the time between the earliest starting date and the latest ending date for all participating stores.

3.4.3 Past Promotional Analysis

Analysing the success or failure of a campaign using historical time series data is referred to as past promotional analysis. The goal of the promotional analysis is to comprehend the impact of previous promotions and formulate future campaigns that can yield profits again.

A good past promotion analysis process should include:

- The ability to measure the success of past promotions for profit increase.
- Measure the difference between incremental category sales vs cannibalistic category sales.
- Allow the decision maker to quickly view the information in an easy-to-understand analysis when needed at the point of making decisions on upcoming promotions.

3.4.4 Promotion Optimisation

The process of optimising retail promotions is quite similar to that of retail pricing. However, instead of submitting an entire category for optimisation with a given set of rules, the retail promotions optimisation process requires the submission of rule sets for each set of planned promotions.

Furthermore, the retail promotion optimisation process is typically a lot more iterative because of the considerations of the vendors and other logistics involved in the process.

When a promotion optimisation is complete, retailers will have the optimal price and the duration for the promotion. However, the duration can be fixed to optimise just for the price as well. The resulting prices will be in compliance with the various rules of the category such as margin rules, product relationships, allowed price discounts and last-digit ending rules.

3.5.5 Trade Negotiations

Retail planning can be a daunting task and often times retailers cannot count on a regular forecast to predict demand when the future conditions of price, promotion or markdown are expected to change the forecast. In these cases, retailers can leverage the coefficients and equations of the models to accurately predict the impact of the price change.

Furthermore, these forecasting capabilities can be leveraged with real-time forecasting capabilities. Imagine a situation where a category manager is on the call with a trade vendor who is offering two options: 20 crates at \$20/piece or 25 crates at \$19/piece. While still on the call, the category manager can quickly forecast for both scenarios and make a wise decision that will allow for maximum efficiency of the promotion being planned.

Needless to say, a well-forecasted promotion can not only provide additional profits for the retailer, but it can also ensure that the customers are getting a discount that they value the most and there is less chance of unsold products or of a stock-out situation.

3.4.6 Test vs Control Process

A test vs control mechanism can be utilised to make better promotion decisions with reduced risks of running an incorrect promotion. For example, a promotion can be tested in a small number of stores before implementing the prices across the entire chain. It is important to note that the smaller number of test stores should be representative of the entire population of stores. This selection of stores for the test can be based on statistical methodologies. Further the results of the test can help improve the promotions with recommendations to either increase or decrease the promoted price before execution across the chain.

3.4.7 Promotions Execution

Executions of promotions can be tricky because they only last for a short duration and involve a lot of work in changing the price labels. Careful store labour planning is necessary to ensure the proper execution of these price changes on time. Often times the POS system will automatically pick up or drop a promoted price as scheduled, but the labels might not reflect this leading to confusion with the customer inside the store.

Many merchants frequently compile a general list of products that will be advertised throughout the entire chain rather than localising promotions. The choice of what will go on end-caps and how it will be merchandised is often left up to the store teams. In many cases, the lack of compliance with the promoted prices on the store labels results in the promotions not reaching their potential.

Efficient promotion execution requires planning for the store labour, inventory, shipping logistics, and auditing processes to ensure quality.

3.4.8 Results Measurement

Running a successful promotion should not only mean increased profits on the promoted products but also increased profits for the entire category. When a customer sees a promotion, this should not cannibalise the sales of another product that would have normally been sold at a regular price. This difference can be measured by looking for "incremental sales" in the entire category or sub-category and checking for "cannibalistic sales" in the same category or sub-category.

A well-run promotion will have the following characteristics:

- This will result in increased sales or profit for the promoted product.
- This will result from incremental sales for the entire subcategory or category.
- Will drive additional traffic to the store.
- Will provide a healthy margin to the vendor supplying the product.
- Will improve the competitive image in the customer's mind.
- Will sell through the planned or purchased inventory level.
- Will sell through before the sell-by date, especially around a holiday or event-specific promotions.

KPIs and dashboards should be built to measure the ability of the promotion to achieve the above-mentioned objectives.

3.5 Post-optimisation Processes and Regulations

Retailers can build certain additional processes and note regulations to ensure the proper extraction of a promotion strategy. This section describes a few of the important aspects in this regard.

3.5.1 Checking Competitive Reactions

While running a promotion is usually a short time internal activity, it is important to note how the competitors are reacting to the retailer's promotion. This is especially true for the highly competitive markets and the image items within these markets.

An aggressively matched promotion at the same time by another competitor can be detrimental to both retailers. By measuring and understanding the behaviour of competitors, retailers can strategically plan future promotions to ensure both profitability and market share growth.

3.5.2 Checking Customer Reactions

The sales data will give the best reading on customer reactions to promotions. However, it might also be a good idea to check with customers through surveys or interactions on how a particular promotion was received.

Retailers can also have sentiment analysis dashboards configured to understand could see how customers are reacting to promotions in online forums and social media. When built, these dashboards automatically update based on consumers' reactions online and make this data available for decision-making by the category managers.

Certain metrics can be leveraged to check for customer reactions. Some of these metrics are discussed below:

Productive Performance Indicator: This metric determines the number of customer orders processed per human hour. To increase productivity, order processing must be done in such a way that processing time is kept to a minimum. Customer service automation strategies can result in immediate improvements in call centre automation, internet ordering, contact management automation, EDIs, and other areas. Because everything is automated, web-integrated customer response systems eliminate the need to hire more employees.

Total Response Cost: The key financial performance indicator is Total Response Cost (TRC). TRC allows organisations to easily calculate the costs incurred for customer responses workflow, assets used, the infrastructure used within the organisation, medium charges such as internet and phone, executive income, and so on. TRC is also used to indicate profitable aspects, such as which responses were profitable and which were not. It can also determine which customers are profitable for the organisation and which are not, as well as which customers can continue to provide more profit in the future. Total response cost is a powerful system that aids in the improvement of an organisation's financial aspects by limiting investments made by the organisation and always keeping a check on customer response to improve financial features.

3.5.3 Promotion Regulations in Europe

Separate rules in all the nations in Europe have hampered efforts to create consistent pan-European campaigns in the sales promotion sector. While the United Kingdom (UK) is an open economy that relies on self-regulation, other nations, like Germany are controlled by regulations that make sales promotion activities difficult (Figure 3.6).

In France, it is illegal to sell at a loss. It has established a resale below cost (RBC) criterion to determine the minimum price at which merchants are permitted to sell a product. Currently, the RBC level is calculated as the product's base purchase price, plus the transportation expenses (to the retailer's warehouse) minus discounts. The government proposed limiting food discounts to 34% of a product's price for 25% of available volumes. This made retailers run promotions, like three products for the price of two – though only for a fourth of their inventory. The reduction of up to 70% resulting from the price war was frequently backed by food producers. The aim of the initiative was to prevent customers from losing their price sensitivity (Reuters).

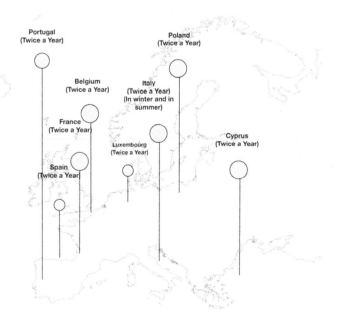

Figure 3.6 Promotional Frequency in Europe.

In June 2018, the UK government prohibited the promotion of high-fat, high-sugar, and high-salt foods (HFSS) based on location and price. Multiply offers and volume promotions, which are common in supermarkets to promote specific products, were phased out under the new law. However, the general price reductions of these products were unaffected. The HFSS regulations required store-level action and many retailers were concerned about revenue loss from prominent promotional locations. Restrictions on store opening hours and on sales below cost can also be one of the main concerns of retailers across the EU.

Regulations imposing taxes, such as property tax, and fees on the retail sector have a significant impact on retailers who use a brick-and-mortar distribution channel. For example, in Belgium, there are local taxes on parking spaces, shop surfaces, and sign sizes. The retail sector in the UK and Ireland is most concerned about business rates. Shop opening hours have not been liberalised in many countries and continue to be a major source of concern for retailers there. In countries like Poland, retailers are concerned about the possibility of regulatory reintroduction. Shop opening hours are not regulated in many places but are limited by labour market regulations.

Sales below cost are heavily regulated, such as in Italy, or prohibited in some countries like Portugal. Thereby limiting the growth of the retail sector.

With regulations differing by country, retailers' concerns in Europe are mostly country-specific. Details of promotional regulations in Europe are given in the following table.

Table 3.1 Retail Promotion Regulations in Europe-2022

Country	Freq/Yr	Length Sales Period	Products Covered	Pre-seasonal Sales/Blackout Conditions that Apply
BE	Twice	3 January–31 January and 1 July 31 July	Merchandise must be held by the seller at the beginning of the sales period and must have been offered for sale at least 30 days before that date.	No announcements of price reductions on clothing, leather goods and shoes during the period of a month before the start of the sales (i.e. 3 December–2 January 2 and 1 June–30 June.
CY	Twice	1 month in 1–28 February, 1 month in 1–31 August	Textile products, footwear, household equipment, and any kind of furniture.	Products have to show the pre-sales and sales prices.
FR	Twice	Max. period of 6 weeks. Precise dates set by authorities.	Merchandise must have been paid for by the retailer and have been offered for sale for at least 1 month before the start of the sale.	Merchandise must have been paid for by the retailer and have been offered for sale for at least 1 month before the start of the sale. Sales below cost are allowed in sales periods.
GR	Four Time	Reg Disc: Second Monday in January to February July until end of August Interim Disc: First 10 days of May and first 10 days of November.	All	

IT	Twice	Varies across country: Regional jurisdiction. Usually 60 days.	Regional jurisdiction. In Emilia Romagna, Friuli Venezia Giulia, Campania and Trento Province, preseason sales are free. In other regions blackouts are applied.
LU	Twice a year	Varies across country: Regional jurisdiction. Usually 60 days.	Non-food (textile and footwear).
LU	Twice a year		
PL	Twice a year	2 weeks each	
PT	Twice a year	28 December–28 February, 15 July–15 September	i Products expressly bought for that purpose may not be sold on sale, being considered to be in that situation all products bought and received in the commercial store for the first time or during the month that precedes the time period of the price reduction ii The merchandise to be sold on sales may not have been under any kind of offer at a lower price or under more favorable terms of purchase in the month preceding the beginning of the sales season

(Continued)

Table 3.1 (Continued)

Country	Freq/Yr	Length Sales Period	Products Covered	Pre-seasonal Sales/Blackout Conditions that Apply
SI	Twice a year	1st working Monday in January and 2nd working Monday in July	Textile products and footwear	
ES	Twice a year	At least 1 week and at most 2 month, at the retailer's discretion	Merchandise must have been offered for sale for at least 1 month and not have been the subject of any promotional activity.	

Chapter 4

Markdown

4.1 Introduction

A markdown is a reduction in the price of an item due to its inability to sell for its original selling price. It is the gap between the initial retail sales price and the actual selling price in a store. Though demand fluctuations are normal and companies can predict seasonal effects – seasonality in retail refers to the regular fluctuations of purchasing patterns throughout the year. However, companies often reduce prices by offering discounts to clear existing stock before launching a new one. This method of stock clearance at the end of a season is called end-of-season markdown.

Markdowns are intended to boost demand for low-demand items for a limited time – till all available stock clears out. Markdowns are nearly always a given. It is impossible to have exactly the right quantity of inventory to meet consumer demand. In fact, most shops prefer to keep some additional inventory than have empty shelves. Therefore, the only way to sell off the surplus inventory is to lower pricing.

Although markdowns and promotions can both increase sales, the goals and approaches of the two price events are different. Retailers need to strategise markdowns to identify what works best for their business.

4.2 Markdown Strategy Formulation

Every product in retail is at a different stage of its lifecycle. While some products are being launched with additional marketing, others are being sold at their regular price, certain products will be promoted to achieve various objectives and other products will need to be discontinued and the floor or shelf space needs to be cleared out for new products.

This chapter will discuss the various components that go into this process of discontinuing the sales of a product while making the most profit or the least loss while clearing out the last inventory available for the discontinued product.

DOI: 10.4324/9781003382140-5

4.2.1 Markdown Strategy

Now that we understand why markdowns are used, let us explore how to create and implement an effective retail markdown strategy. A retail markdown strategy is critical since it directly affects sales growth and stock disposal. Without a discount plan, retailers may find themselves with over-stocked store shelves, reduced sales numbers, and a loss of purchasing power. The retailers will not be able to introduce new products into the assortment if the shelves are packed with idle inventory. A discount plan is also an efficient technique to attract more people to the retail business. This gives the opportunity to sell more to the existing customers and perhaps also to drive a favourable image of being a low-priced retailer. Figure 4.1 shows what needs to be considered to make an effective markdown strategy.

- Being Proactive: Retailers do not want to be stuck with products that are not selling since. After all, the inventory is expenditure. Before a selling season begins, strategies need to be in place to mark down the products and communicate and educate the employees on how to go about it.
- Defining Goals: Whether to dispose of unsold merchandise, recover the initial investment, or attract a specific type of customer, retailers need to identify the purpose or goal to offer a discount or markdown a product.
- Reviewing Past Data: The POS system is the best friend of a retailer. It reveals a quick performance of the previous season, the inventory remaining after a previous markdown, and whether or not it was effective. With this information, retailers can start planning the next markdown. It can also help enhance the purchasing strategy in the future.
- Considering Pricing Strategy: Every product in the business is priced in one of three categories: budget, value, or luxury. This is important to know how to price products for optimising short-term sales, and know what the customer wants and values while maintaining the brand image.
- Understanding KPIs: When a KPI trend is in the wrong direction, intervening quickly can help to mitigate the trend's negative financial consequences.

Markdown Strategy

| Being Proactive | Defining Goals | Reviewing Past Data | Considering Pricing Strategy | Understanding KPIs | Agile Pricing |

Figure 4.1 Making a Markdown Strategy.

In other words, identifying the issue before it escalates into a flood of cash streaming out of the company. Finally, retailers should keep in mind that retail stores do not exist in a vacuum. In most circumstances, they will be surrounded by competitors who are all vying for a larger piece of the sales or market share. Monitoring KPIs isn't optional if retailers want to keep (or enhance) the store's competitive position.

- Agile Pricing: A technique known as agile pricing keeps the price points flexible so that retailers can quickly match or undercut the competition. This approach helps boost sales and overall revenue if a competitor runs out of a certain product having high demand.

4.2.2 Markdown Types

There are two types of markdowns that are observed in the retail industry. The first is clearance markdown. This is when a retailer does not intend to replenish an item. Especially when it will be cost-effective to sell the item at a discount rather than pay for its storage. Thus, clearance markdowns increase sales by lowering the price of a product thereby allowing surplus inventory to be sold off faster. Essentially, it is meant to get rid of excess inventory in a store.

The other is damaged goods markdown. This is when a product unit is damaged and is unlikely to get sold at its original intended price. It is a common practice to lower the price of any damaged product with manufacturing defects.

For implementing markdowns, it is necessary to examine certain considerations carefully. Figure 4.2 depicts an overview of the considerations, described in detail in the subsequent sections.

4.3 Science of Markdowns

The science and the models used for markdown are again similar to that of retail pricing however there are several key differences that need to be considered during the markdown modelling and optimisation process.

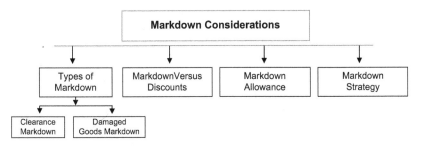

Figure 4.2 Markdown Considerations in the Retail Sector.

4.3.1 Discount Response Modelling

Modelling for markdown is a process quite similar to modelling for pricing. Most of the data input remains the same in terms of the Retailer provided and Market sourced data. However, the markdown models need additional data input in terms of real-time inventory data, salvage value, sell-by dates, allowed percentage discounts, and time between two different prices.

The modelling team here should carefully consider the nuances of customer behaviour when it comes to markdown pricing. Time plays an important factor in many cases. For example, a 50% discount on a holiday coffee mug before the holiday holds a very different value when compared to the same discount after the holiday. Further, a very steep discount might signify that there is a possibility that the product was of inferior quality or damaged in the customer's mind. Add to this, the retailer often imposes a condition that products on markdown or clearance cannot be returned.

Given these factors, retailers should make note that the coefficients for elasticity are quite different and handled differently than a regular price or promotion discount. Furthermore, these coefficients should be recalculated and updated on a weekly basis during the execution of the markdown for better results.

4.3.2 Factors Involved in Markdowns

In a world where most retailers place purchase orders with their suppliers many months before the season, accurate forecasting of future customer needs and preferences is essential. To maximise sales and margins, successful retail planners must balance product risks, predict competitive offerings, be aware of the macroeconomic landscape that can impact costs and international markets, and estimate the right buy quantities. Many factors need to be considered during a markdown process, some of them are described below:

4.3.2.1 Cannibalisation Effect

When a newly released product pulls demand away from existing products within the same portfolio, it is referred to as product cannibalisation. Often seen in the retail environment, this effect caused by the new product results in a loss of sales and money. Instead of poaching customers, revenue, and market share from external competitors, this occurrence fosters internal competition between items. This condition, which is usually unanticipated, can disrupt sales and cause overstocking of existing products, inventory imbalances, and extreme markdowns. The silver lining is that there are several triggers leading to product cannibalism, which can be identified and corrected.

4.3.2.2 Salvage Value

The estimated resale worth of a product at the end of its useful life is known as salvage value. In many cases, retailers might have agreements with the vendors on the cost at which a vendor is willing to take back unsold products. In other cases, retailers might have agreements with other retailers who might have agreements to buy unsold products on a periodic basis at a lower cost. A retailer might also have a last resort agreement to donate, scrap or recycle unsold products for a small revenue or tax benefits. The final value that can be obtained by a product that remains unsold on a retailer's shelf is the Salvage Value of the product and this forms an important part of the markdown modelling process.

4.3.2.3 Sell-By Dates

For retailers, the sell-by date indicates when a product needs to be sold or re-moved from the shelf for sale. This can be based on many factors such as:

- Product expiration dates
- End of seasons
- Holiday dates
- New product release dates
- Assortment or planogram reset dates

4.3.2.4 Markdown Allowance

Retailers often negotiate with suppliers or manufacturers to provide a markdown allowance to cover expenses incurred by the retailer selling the vendor's prod-ucts. This is done to offset any possible losses in the case of faulty products and prevent unexpected markdowns.

Thus, retailers and vendors share their inventory and sales risk. Many man-ufacturing companies provide even credit to retailers if the latter are unsure about selling the products and prefer to have security for the sales.

However, many large and well-established manufacturers do not prefer to give such allowances perhaps due to the power of their brand image amongst the consumer and also perhaps due to the negotiation power larger vendors inher-ently possess.

4.3.3 Customer Behaviour with Markdowns

From Black Friday and Cyber Monday sales to Memorial Day and Fourth of July sales, retailers have trained customers to look for deals all year. This strategy has significantly altered consumer purchasing behaviour, causing the average shopper to become more price sensitive and selective in their purchases.

Customers might be more willing to look for deeply discounted clearance sales from online websites which could be a channel the retailers can use for their markdown sales, perhaps under a different brand name or a retail partner who can handle clearing the unwanted products online.

While certain consumers might become wary of deep discounts and associate them with quality perceptions, others might wait and hunt the products on clearance. This is important to note as it differs by product type, location and time of the year. Leveraging the information from this analysis can allow retailers to make better markdown decisions and perhaps address the needs of the different customer segments in silos to provide the most customer value while making better margins.

4.4 Markdown Process

4.4.1 Markdown Data Infrastructure

The data infrastructure needed for markdowns is similar to the data requirements of a base pricing model. However, the data infrastructure should carry information about the inventory levels at the product store level in real-time, the sell-by dates, the salvage value, and also about the rules of markdown such as allowed price discounts and time between markdowns.

4.4.2 Markdown Identification/Pareto/Space Allocation

Retailers know, from the time they plan their inventory, they will sell some of their inventory at full price at first, then subject it to various levels of markdowns until it is cleared. Figure 4.3 shows the markdown process.

A Pareto analysis can be used to identify the products that are contributing the least amount to the overall sales or profit in a retail assortment. This analysis should be performed at a lower product aggregation level such as the sub-category level

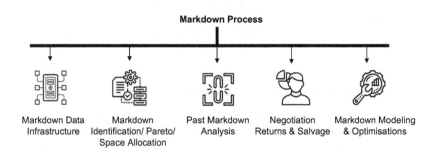

Figure 4.3 Markdown Process.

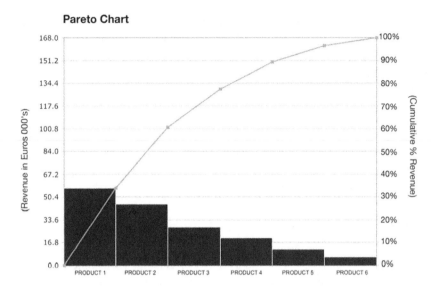

Pareto Chart

Figure 4.4 Pareto Chart.

and filtered by geographic regions. A product that is selling well in one region of the country might not be doing well in another part.

It is typical to see a high percentage of sales come from a smaller percentage of the assortment. This spread can be visualised using the Pareto analysis. In many cases a category that hasn't been carefully managed might have a "long tail", meaning many products contribute almost nothing to the overall revenue and assortment and may for the list of prime candidates to be discontinued. However, care should be exercised to not discontinued essential products that may still be low volume. (Figure 4.4).

4.4.3 Markdown Identification Process

A good markdown process requires many standard steps that need to be performed by multiple parts of the pricing organisation.

Identifying the proper items to mark down and when to mark them down would be based on the sales performance of the products, the strategic goals and the resource considerations. Retailers may identify "stars" and "dogs" in their portfolio by integrating in-season item performance data with the item's plan using a simple visualisation tool. As a consequence, retailers may identify which products are performing well and can be held back from clearing, as well as which items are failing and should be marked down more rapidly in order to maximise profits.

To determine the ideal markdown plan, retailers and planners must use consumer-centric analytics and pre-set business rules to determine the appropriate discount amount. An ideal clearance price for the products recognised by retailers through visualisation may be discovered using simple techniques to optimise gross margins and sell-through, subject to a set of business rules or limitations.

Subsequently, consumer demand analytics are used to forecast the projected sales pattern and financial impact of implementing the ideal clearance price. This advanced analytics technique generates convincing and plain rationale that retailers and planners may evaluate before acting. These analytics may be used by retailers and planners to do scenario assessments on pricing and markdown timing to maximise their overall returns.

4.4.4 Past Markdown Analysis

Retailers can analyse historical data to identify trends of their own markdowns and what went well and what did not. It can help them examine trends of markdowns and subsequent surplus inventory they may have had. This can help them take corrective action.

For example, if a retailer sold out stocks of a product too quickly in the previous year, the store can postpone markdowns for a few weeks in the current year to increase profits. Thus, historical data can aid in determining whether goods require a price adjustment and when markdowns should be applied. Retailers who discount too much, too quickly, risk losing money and running out of stock. Retailers who do not discount products or wait too long to do so might lose money and end up with excess inventory. Further, retailers can also leverage data from historical markdowns to find out the demand response patterns of their customers and how they may be differing with geography and time dimensions.

4.4.5 Negotiation Returns and Salvage

Unsold products from a retailer need to be gotten rid of to make room for products that can sell from the same space. While running a markdown is one way to get rid of unwanted products, retailers can have other mechanisms to clear out unwanted inventory as well.

- Retailers can have pre-negotiated agreements with vendors to return the unsold products at cost or at a lower price.
- Retailers can have agreements with other retailers to take on the unsold inventory. For example, a mid-tier fashion retailer might have an agreement with a discount retailer to take over unsold inventory at the end of a season.

- Retailers can have agreements with companies that recycle products and materials as scrap.
- Retailers can arrange for unsold products to be donated which might also allow them to claim certain tax benefits.

The term "Salvage value" for the purposes of our analytical modelling refers to the price a retailer would get through any channel other than his own retail sales. This is an important input for the markdown modelling and optimisation processes.

4.4.6 Markdown Modelling and Optimisations

Markdown modelling examines the historical performance of products. A markdown model can provide equations and coefficients that can be leveraged to understand, optimise, predict and measure markdowns. Markdown models have a core set of variables that could include Seasonality, Lifecycle, Trends, Demand Elasticity, Cross Elasticity and Competitive Factors.

4.4.6.1 Markdown Optimisation

Markdown optimisation, primarily, strategically lowers a product's sell price by identifying the correct timing and the extent of markdown required. It takes into account factors such as a product's historical sales, characteristics, price range, competitors' pricing, store characteristics, and seasonality trends.

Figure 4.5 shows the various factors considered in optimising markdowns. Let us look at these factors in detail:

Scheduling Markdowns: The schedule for markdowns needs to be made based on several considerations. Some of them are listed below:

- The sell-by dates for the products being considered for Markdown.
- The store labour availability for changing prices.
- Upcoming holidays and events that might affect the demand for a product.

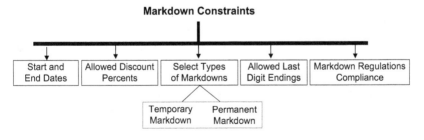

Figure 4.5 Markdown Constraints.

- The time between different markdown discounts is allowed both from a process and legal standpoint.

Deciding the Price Drop: Reduced-price or markdowns are perceived by consumers as a percentage off the original or regular retail price of the product. Whereas, for retailers, it is an adjustment of its monetary value or price. Retailers need to decide on the quantity or percentage of price reduction and implement the markdown on time to match the consumers' expectations of the product value. It is a common practice for a shop to start with a 20% to 25% discount and sell as many products as possible at that price. If the sales do not pick up even then, the prices are further dropped by 33%, and finally to one-half of the retail price or less. Through an analytics-based markdown optimisation process, these discount percentages and schedules may be determined scientifically to max-imising the results based on the strategic objectives.

The percentage of Markdown sales can be determined by using the following formulae:

$$\text{Markdown \%} = \text{Markdown (\$)} \div \text{Net Sale (\$)}$$
$$\text{Net Sales (\$)} = \text{Retail Price (\$)} \times \text{Units Sold (at each price point)}$$

Last Digit Endings: Retailers may allow only certain digits for a markdown price. These sets of last digits are determined based on the range of the prices. For example, while a .49, .75, and .99 might be allowed for all price points below $5. Only .99 may be allowed for all price points above $10. In some cases, retailers use a certain last digit, such as .07 or .08 to indicate that the product is at a clearance price.

Regulation Compliance: In the European Union, prices of a product can be compared with their equivalent in the neighbouring countries due to the free movement of goods, the elimination of customs barriers, and the harmonisation of value-added tax (VAT) rates. Retailers have typically established a number of markdown policies to limit markdowns and use them to run a more lucrative business. Some of these ideas are as follows:

- A valid relationship exists between a product and the period of the selling season during which it is discounted. Fashion goods, for example, change often. As a result, markdowns cannot be delayed until the end of the selling season, especially if the shop wants to sell trendy products when the buyer is interested. Fashion items do not improve with age.
- The type of retailer and method of distribution influence the timing of markdowns.
- The first markdown is generally the least expensive to the store if the goods are lowered enough to quickly attract the target buyer.

- The initial markdown must be made early enough in the selling season to allow for additional markdowns on the items later in the selling season.
- The amount of the discount is determined by the original retail price and the time of the decrease. Retailers must be careful not to cut too quickly and determine the price of goods the buyers will pay at this point in the selling season.
- Markdowns should be done in dollar increments. The first markdown is generally 25% or 14 off of the original retail price; the second markdown is usually 33% and 1/3% or 1/3 off of the original retail price, and the third markdown is usually 50% or 12 of the retail price.

Another policy influencing lower goods sales is how the business stores the merchandise. Markdown products should be arranged, merchandised, and promoted in the same way that regular markets do. Markdown products should also be kept separate from regular-priced merchandise. Clear signage indicating the type of reduction is a common quiet selling strategy used by retailers.

The primary objective of retail markdown optimisation remains to dispose of excess and underutilised inventory. Retailers use markdown optimisation techniques to ensure that their inventory and assortment are optimally aligned with consumer demand. Fluctuating product life cycles, seasonal demands, varied assortments, customer diversity, new stores, and price competition, among others, may alter the process of markdown optimisations.

Markdown optimisation helps avoid overstocking and products reaching sell-by dates and work out the best price to clear the stock and maximise profit.

4.4.6.2 Markdown Optimisation Process

A well-planned markdown optimisation process calls for five key steps:

1   Define Markdown Optimisation Strategy: Markdown optimisation and the price strategy, as well as the markdown plan and targets, are the two most crucial aspects to specify. A good pricing strategy needs to define the minimum and maximum markdown rates allowed and the level of optimisation desired. Markdown goals are a higher-level decision: should optimisations be calculated to maximise margin or to clear remaining stock? For both pricing strategy and markdown plan and goals, the solution needs to be flexible. A company needs to be able to optimise pricing at any level, whether a product or even product location and change campaign goals if required.
2   Identify Markdown Products Correctly: When retailers try to manually identify items without using automation, it is already too late. The strategy should be to avoid marking down a product beyond its expiration dates and well before the new inventory arrives.

3 Optimise Prices as per Strategy: A markdown optimisation system runs markdown optimisation software to calculate discount schedules for merchants. Furthermore, the markdown optimisation system employs methodologies to consistently approximate and quantify the value gained by a specific store by implementing a calculated markdown plan rather than a user-defined schedule. A markdown optimisation system computes the best pricing for markdown products automatically. These computations adhere to the markdown strategy's criteria and limitations (minimum and maximum price adjustments, level of optimisation, among others). All this is in keeping with the campaign goal – which may be maximising margin or clearing stock by the termination date.

4 Convert Recommendations into Actions: A markdown optimisation system shows products that are missing their sales objectives and items with forecasted stock balances as their product life cycle approaches its end. The exception view provides the best pricing for each of those goods, based on the company's markdown policy.

5 Monitoring Campaign Performance: When discount planning and execution are done manually, monitoring a campaign may get neglected as planners focus on more pressing matters. Markdown optimisation makes even a campaign success analysis easier with dashboards that provide inventory forecasts, predicted end balances by termination dates, and a comparison of goal versus achieved gross profit and margin.

4.4.6.3 Managing Markdown Optimisation

When retailers have the right technology in place to evaluate and manage markdowns and related price concerns, they can achieve the following important goals:

- Make corrections to the markdown schedule in terms of duration and discount levels as needed.
- Allocate resources or move inventory between stores if need be.
- Avoid empty shelves and re-organise shelf space if needed.
- Evaluate the link between price elasticity and inventory with improved decision-making using reliable technologies.
- Make future decisions that lead to the greatest outcomes for their operations by having a useful insight into price degradation.
- Measure the Gross Margin Return On Investment (GMROI).

4.4.6.4 Networked Learning Models

Markdowns often run based on different price discount levels in different stores for the same product. This is largely because the Markdown discount percent depends on the amount of inventory left with respect to the sell-by date. When the markdown coefficients are recalculated every week, there is an opportunity to "learn" better coefficients from the other stores which might have run the markdown at a different rate.

Furthermore, the inventory from one store can be shipped to nearby stores to balance the inventory of the products, allowing both stores to sell at a lesser discounted level. This requires the cost of shipping and other logistics such as the cost of labour, transport, and storage to be calculated.

Planning for the logistics of the intrachain transportation of unsold merchandise can allow for incremental profits and faster sales over time. However, it is important to note that retailers usually have a well-oiled machine to ship products from the warehouse to the retail stores and not necessarily between nearby stores. Perhaps, the retailers can explore a "ship back" to utilise the empty delivery trucks that could take the unsold markdown inventory back to the warehouse, from where these products can find a place in the store where they are actually selling.

4.4.6.5 Markdown with Advertising

With the knowledge of the Markdown Discount percentage, various advertising and marketing activities can be coordinated with the discount schedule for maximum impact. The Markdown Discount percentage is calculated as follows:

$$\text{Markdown Discount\%} = ([\text{Original Price} - \text{Sales Price}]/\text{Original Price}) \times 100$$

So, if you sell a TV for $300 that was originally priced at $500, your markdown percentage is:

$$([\$500 - \$300 / \$500) \times 100 = 40\%$$

4.5 Post-markdown Processes and Regulations

Retailers can build certain additional processes and note regulations to ensure the proper execution of a markdown strategy. This section describes a few of the important aspects in this regard.

4.5.1 Execution and Weekly Revisions

Retailers plan expected markdown schedules and amounts for products considering their life cycles to avoid last-minute extreme price drops. Higher demand at lower discount levels can ensure higher margins.

Markdown timing is not a set formula. It varies by product, market, and even store. A typical markdown schedule for TV is shown in Figure 4.6. Instead of waiting for the end of product life, companies can schedule a series of markdowns

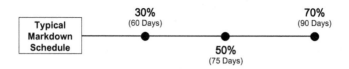

Figure 4.6 Typical Markdown Schedule.

based on their assortment and the seasonality of their categories. New television stock-keeping units (SKUs) can sustain demand for up to a year, whereas fast fashion clothing SKUs need to be cleared in 60 days. For televisions, a store may reduce prices in the sixth month of its launch, then again in the ninth month, and finally at its year-end, just before a new model is about to be released. However, depending on factors like markdown performance, holidays, events and store labour, a company may modify the timing and size of markdowns.

4.5.2 Results Measurement

The process of measuring results is similar to the ones in promotions. The difference here is the total profitability should depend on the salvage value and sometimes the primary goal is not profit maximisation, but attaining the maximum possible revenue to clear out the shelf space in time for the new assortment. In this case, the cost is not really an important factor in the measurement of success.

The sales due to a markdown process are subject to huge variations and need to be monitored very closely. Not only can the price points be different by location for the same product, but these prices should also be changing regularly – perhaps weekly. It is important to monitor these markdowns and make any changes to the prices or even the location of the markdown – through inter-store inventory shipping.

Many KPIs can be built to track these markdowns by including metrics on profitability, sell-through rates, and projected leftover inventory by sell-by dates.

4.5.3 Markdown Regulations

In most cases, once a retailer declares an item as a markdown or clearance, the product should not be sold again in the store after the clearance sale is complete.

For example, the regulations around former price comparisons as amended on 28 December 2022 by the Code of Federal Regulations in the United States are as followed:

a   One of the most common types of bargain advertising is to offer a discount off the advertiser's previous price for an article. If the former price is the genuine, regular price at which the article was offered to the public on a regular basis for a reasonable period of time, it provides a legitimate basis for advertising a price comparison. Where the former price is genuine, the advertised bargain is genuine. If, on the other hand, the former price being advertised is fictitious rather than genuine – for example, where an artificially inflated price was established in order to enable the subsequent offer of a large reduction – the advertised "bargain" is false; the purchaser does not receive the unusual value he expects. In this case, the "reduced" price is most likely just the seller's regular price.

b   A former price is not necessarily fictitious simply because no sales were made at the advertised price. However, in such a case, the advertiser should be especially cautious that the price is one at which the product was openly and actively offered for sale, for a reasonably substantial period of time, in the recent, regular course of his business, honestly and in good faith – and, of course, not for the purpose of establishing a fictitious higher price on which a deceptive comparison could be based. And the advertiser should avoid any implication that a previous price is a selling price rather than an asking price unless substantial sales at that price were actually made.

c   Here's an example of a price comparison based on a fictitious previous price. John Doe is a seller of Brand X fountain pens for $5 each. His usual markup is 50% above cost, so his regular retail price is $7.50. Doe begins selling Brand X at $10 per pen in order to offer an unusual "bargain" later on. He realises that at this inflated price, he will be able to sell none or very few pens. But he doesn't mind because he only keeps that price for a few days. Then he "cuts" the price to $7.50 and advertises: "Terrific Bargain: X Pens, Were $10, Now only $7.50!" This is clearly a false claim. The advertised "bargain" is a forgery.

d   Other examples of fictitious price comparisons could be provided. An advertiser may use a price at which he never offered the article at all; he may use a price that was not used in the regular course of business, or that was not used recently but at some distant period in the past, without disclosing that fact; he may use a price that was not openly offered to the public, or that was not maintained for a reasonable length of time but was immediately reduced.

e   If the former price is stated in the advertisement, whether or not it is accompanied by descriptive terminology such as "Regularly", "Usually", "Formerly", and so on, the advertiser should ensure that the former price is not fictitious. If the previous price, or the amount or percentage of reduction, is not stated in the advertisement, such as when the ad simply states, "Sale", the advertiser must ensure that the amount of reduction is not so minor that it is meaningless. It should be large enough that the consumer if he knew what it was, would believe he was getting a genuine bargain or saving. An advertiser who claims that an item has been "Reduced to $9.99" when the previous price was $10 is misleading the consumer, who will interpret the claim to mean that a much larger, rather than merely nominal, a reduction was offered.

Source: Code of Federal Regulations (Section 233.1)

4.5.4 Reducing Food Waste

An important reason for markdowns in case of food and especially fresh produce is to reduce food waste. About 5% to 20% of all food sold in a retail establishment is wasted because a retailer is unable to sell the product before it reaches its expiration date or has decomposed. This percentage of waste is significantly higher in less developed retail systems.

Wasted food is not only a loss of revenue for the retailer, but it is also a significant cause of Global Warming which is having a catastrophic effect on our environment. The decomposed food often emits Methane, which is a significant contributor to Global warming.

While many retailers often take many steps with both profit-oriented and altruistic intentions to reduce food waste through well-planned Markdowns, in many cases the reduction in food waste is mandated by various government agencies as well. In some cases, the retailers and the country itself get several taxes and other benefits from the world governing bodies to incentivise food waste reduction in retail.

Retailers may partner with local food produce donation agencies to find a hungry stomach for food that will not sell in time but is still healthy to consume.

Retailers might also leverage many technology innovations being developed to detect the stage of life of the fresh produce or fresh food and connect it with automated algorithms to price, perhaps on Electronic Shelf Labels (ESLs) for reduction of food waste through automated markdowns.

4.5.5 Strategy and Image Protection

While pricing is an important lever to get rid of unwanted merchandise, careful consideration should also be paid to the image the lower priced products will project amongst its consumers. A lower price can certainly drive traffic and increase demand, but in certain cases such as on Fresh Produce or products that are positioned to be of high quality, a lower price can be detrimental to increasing demand for a product. In such cases, retailers can use additional tactics to address the task of a markdown, this could include:

- Adding additional messaging to signify that the discount is being applied to a product that is ready to be consumed immediately.
- This is the retailer working to reduce food waste and the customer could help participate in this.
- Choosing a separate place in the retail store, such as a markdown corner or shelf so the value-conscious customers or the customers who do not associate the lower price with the lower quality can go and shop in that section.
- Selling through a separate brand, partner or channel – such as online – for the deeply discounted sales.

4.5.6 Avoiding Future Markdowns

While markdown is an essential component of retailing to get rid of unsold inventory and clear the shelf space for new assortment, markdowns can be reduced to a large extent through careful and systematic planning and processes.

For example products likely to be marked down should be identified many months in advance through various analyses that can be configured on the business intelligence platforms. By running a regular promotion at the store level, perhaps automatically, retailers can reduce the amount of inventory level carried before deciding to stop ordering the product from the vendor and then deciding to run a markdown.

Furthermore, as noted earlier, prior agreements can be negotiated with vendors to buy back unsold products at an agreed price so that the retailer can reduce the risk of carryout out a costly markdown process.

Chapter 5

Competitive Pricing

5.1 Introduction

Competitive pricing is an essential part of the retail pricing strategy. The level of competition often depends on the maturity level of a market and the uniqueness of the products being sold in the retail establishment.

While the overall goal of a competitive pricing strategy will depend on many factors, examining the competition and coming up with a strategy to thrive in the market environment is always essential. Both brand manufacturers and retailers aim to achieve a larger piece of the market so that they can reap the benefits of the economies of scale in operations, marketing expenditure and other logistics. A larger market share also facilitates better negotiations with the suppliers thus accommodating a larger profit margin.

5.2 Identifying the Competition

The idea of who your competitors are is often different for a retailer when compared to what the customers see as competing options. While a retailer is most likely to assume that the largest player in its retail market might be its number one competitor, the data might show that the number one competitor might actually be a smaller store which could also be very different in each market. Furthermore, the number one competitor might be different in each category and location. For example, while an online retail giant might be a significant competitor for an electronics retailer in a suburban store, the store downtown might have a small convenience format across from the customer's office to be its largest competitor.

Research is the foundation of an effective competitor-based pricing strategy. Retailers can set prices for the product or service based on an understanding of how the top rivals in the market price their items and how that pricing may affect buyers' expectations.

Figure 5.1 represents the various parameters in competitive pricing to be considered by retailers: who is the business competing with, what they are competing with, and what is the degree of competition.

DOI: 10.4324/9781003382140-6

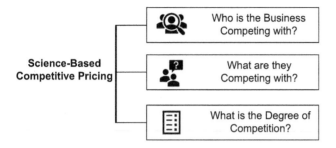

Figure 5.1 Science-Based Competitive Pricing.

Let us look at the three parameters of competitive pricing closely in the following sections.

5.2.1 Who Is the Business Competing With?

Retailers need to be aware of both indirect and direct competition when developing their pricing plan. There are three techniques each for identifying direct and indirect competitors. Let us take a look at these techniques.

5.2.1.1 Direct Competitors

To identify direct competitors for the company, start with the product and the value it gives to its target customers. Here are the three strategies for identifying direct competitors:

- Conduct Market Research: Examine the market for the goods then determine which other businesses are selling a product that is similar to yours. Speak with the rival retailers' sales staff that manages the sales process. Over time, retailers will understand their rivals better, know about their products and marketing activities, and devise ways to outperform them.
- Solicit Customer Feedback: Customers, once again, are the key to defeating the immediate competition. After they have decided on the company and product, retailers can inquire about the other companies and goods. Customers sometimes uncover competitors who could be previously unknown to retailers. Additionally, a retailer's sales team may ask potential consumers which businesses they prefer to buy from and why. If customers have not settled on the product yet, knowing which businesses or goods they are contemplating will help the team better understand their needs.
- Use Social Media: Look for online communities or community forums on social media. Retailers' potential consumers frequently seek information and recommendations on social media sites and applications, and on community

forums such as Quora and Reddit. Retailers may learn more about the competition by looking into the interactions their customers make on these platforms.

5.2.1.2 Indirect Competitors

Retailers' indirect competitors have just as much influence as direct competitors on their pricing process. In fact, because their indirect competitors frequently create material that competes with them, they have an even higher impact on potential buyers early on in the buyer's journey. Here are three techniques on how you can find them:

- Conduct Keyword Research: One simple way to identify indirect competitors is to conduct keyword research on the internet. Retailers can establish which company or publishers are fighting for space on Google by conducting a competitive search engine optimisation (SEO) analysis. Countless potential customers use search engines to find products and services. For today's marketer, this means that the business is up against not only direct competitors, but also every other website on the internet.
- Examining Results: Many indirect competitors are writing about themes similar to the value proposition. Retailers may uncover keywords that are crucial to their product or offering by looking at the value proposition of the product. Then, using Google's search engine results page (SERP), examine who is competing with the material in search engines. Any individual, blog, business, publication, or organisation that creates content around the value proposition is an indirect competitor of the company!
- Analysing Paid Data: Analyse data that has been paid for. Visit AdWords and look out for keywords related to the business. Adwords is a Google-created online advertising platform where marketers compete to display short commercials, service offerings, product listings, or videos to web visitors. It may insert adverts in search engine results like Google Search (the Google Search Network) as well as non-search websites, mobile applications, and videos. Services are priced using a pay-per-click (PPC) basis. Check out the competition for any of those keywords. Look into businesses or websites purchasing advertisements for those keywords. Websites that pay for sponsored space on the search engine results page for a keyword are competing for space on Google with that business's content.

5.2.2 What Are They Competing With?

Retailers cannot determine the price of their products based on their entire assortment. Through careful analysis of past data and other strategic considerations, retailers should determine the set of products on which they will choose to be competitive. The selection of this product set should depend on the following factors:

- Sensitiveness of the demand based on the price for the product (Price Elasticity).
- The volume of sales for this product.
- Is this product an important component of the typical market basket?
- Importance of a product in the competitor's assortment.

Usually, the set of products on which a retailer will base its competitive strategy should not be more than 5% to 10% of the entire assortment.

5.2.3 What Is the Degree of Competition?

In a free enterprise economy, market structures characterise the nature or degree of competition among businesses in the same industry. For perfect competition to exist in the market, certain conditions are required which are as follows:

- A large number of buyers and sellers.
- All dealing in identical products.
- Buyers and sellers need to act independently and compete with one another.
- Both buyers and sellers need to be well-informed of market conditions.
- Both buyers and sellers need to be able to enter and exit the market at any time.

As we can be deduced from the five requirements for an "ideal competition", there is none. Generally, the market structure is described as "imperfect" if any of the five characteristics is not met.

5.2.3.1 The 5D Competitive Matrix

It is important to measure, understand and leverage these varying degrees of competition. Retailers should not compete based on corporate market share level data or rivalry but instead, pay attention to the 5 Dimensions of the competitive matrix to make competitive decisions.

Modelling the volume of a retailer against its competitor's prices can result in several valuable insights. The model needs to be robust enough both technically and with the amount of data supplied to it so that it takes into account the effects of seasonality, trends, and other factors before imputing the impact of a competitor against its own volume of sales.

When done correctly these models can give us a five-dimensional view of the competition with coefficients (or weights) being defined for each of the following competitive metrics.

- Who Matters?
- By How Much?

- On Which Products?
- In Which Markets?
- At What Times?

The results of the above analysis might point out for example that a particular smaller retailer is highly significant in the fresh produce category for the Swiss markets particularly in the summer months. Each of these factors when applied back to quantifiable metrics in the pricing process, will result in a much more streamlined competitive pricing mechanism. The retailer does not lose margin unnecessarily to become the least priced or drop its price to match a competitive price in every case. Instead, the retailer can provide a better competitive image and market share while keeping both the vendors and its customers satisfied.

5.3 Competitive Pricing

While the simplest approach might be to match the prices of the largest player in the market, this is most definitely not the most efficient way to address competitive pricing. The correct approach to competitive pricing will involve several methodical steps performed in order to achieve the desired outcomes in profit, image, vendor and customer satisfaction.

5.3.1 Competitive Pricing Objectives

For pricing a product or service, businesses have three options: to keep their prices below the competitor's price, at the competitor's price, or above the competitor's price. Pricing above the competitor's prices is usually done when the product is superior to that of the competitor and the company is confident of the quality being offered. However, if a business observes that once a consumer has been exposed to the competitor's goods, the customer is likely to purchase the products from them, it may set the price below market, and perhaps even lose money. The profits from the company's other products may then be used to compensate for the loss on the below-market-priced product. This is also known as a loss leader strategy. The third objective may be when a company might opt to charge the same price as that of its competitors (also called price matching) or accept the current market pricing. Even if the company sells the same product at the same price, it may try to differentiate its product through marketing. (Figure 5.2).

After conducting thorough research of the market and the existing competition, retailers have the following three options for pricing their products: as observed in Figure 5.3.

Pricing Above the Competition: Providing items or services at a lower higher cost than the competitors. It is frequently done when retailers believe their products or services are superior to those offered by the competitors.

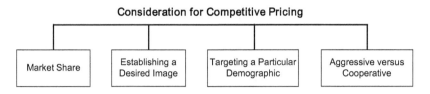

Figure 5.2 Considerations for Competitive Pricing.

Figure 5.3 Competitive Pricing Framework Strategies.

Pricing on the Same Level: Also called Price matching, is another term for the same thing. Retailers' product is priced their products close to similar to that of the competitors. However, even if the product and features are similar to those of the competitors, the primary focus should be on the added value the product provides.

Pricing Below the Competition: If the company's products are limited in terms of features and functionality, the pricing can be below the competitors should not be a strategy. This strategy can also be used when a company wishes to attract clients' customers' attention by offering competitive pricing in order to enhance sales and brand value market share.

5.3.1.1 Gaining Market Share

This is perhaps the toughest strategy to follow. To achieve this, a company needs to pursue the following:

Product (or Service) Innovation: A company can capture a large share of a market if it has a technology, a unique product or an innovation to offer. Delivering new technologies to the market that competitors have yet to provide are all examples of innovation. This way, a company can get an advantage over its competitors and dominate the industry.

Lowering Pricing: This can also help a company gain market share. Lowering prices will draw more customers, allowing a company to grow its customer base and revenues, thereby increasing its market share.

Strengthening Customer Relationships: By safeguarding their existing market and maintaining an existing customer base with good customer communication and relationships. This increases customer satisfaction, which leads to an increase in the customer base through verbal marketing.

Effective Advertising: This is an expensive but successful method of increasing market share. To beat fierce rivalry in the market, advertising is a wonderful strategy to acquire a competitive advantage.

Increased Quality: Customers today are concerned about a product's quality and its pricing. A company's market share can be increased by ensuring greater quality standards.

Making Acquisitions: Buying out a competitor is a sure-fire way to gain control of the industry. By acquiring a competitor, a corporation gains access to a new customer base while also eliminating competition. Thereby establishing dominance over the industry and increasing market share.

5.3.1.2 Establishing the Desired Image

The consumers' perceptions of a retailer's prices in relation to the competition are referred to as price image. It is more of psychological knowledge of a retailer's position in the minds of shoppers than where their pricing actually falls. It has to do with things like prestige pricing (or image pricing) and the brand's reputation.

Big-Ticket Items: Big-ticket items that are highly-priced, high value or expensive products with high-profit margins may play a significant role in the pricing image. This could be because the most expensive things are frequently the most advertised and prominent in a store (physical or online). They get the greatest displays and promotions.

The reputation of the Brand: The brand's reputation also significantly influences the price image. This is frequently associated with channels such as dollar stores, big-box retailers, or luxury stores on a daily basis. When entering into a dollar store as opposed to a high-end apparel designer, shoppers have an internal bias about the prices to expect. Of course, retailers can influence their brand's reputation to some extent by disseminating marketing and sales messages that reflect the image they wish to project.

Stores on the Ground: On a similar point, the actual physical store, notably its design, cleanliness, and layout, is another factor in price image. Customers visiting large stores such as Walmart or Target, may have a preconceived notion of how the pricing will be. A niche store or a "mom-and-pop" shop is in the same boat. Beyond the design, store cleanliness, whether deliberate or not, plays a significant effect. A messy store with empty shelves has a specific pricing image, and the opposite is true.

Discounts and Special Offers: Finally, discounts and promotions have an impact on a brand's or retailer's perceived pricing image. For example, a store that offers frequent discounts on its merchandise can develop a consistent image among its customers. On the other hand, a store that never marks down has a different image. This is also related to price-based advertising. Publicising prices, sales, and events communicate a price image to customers. Offering a price-match guarantee might also help improve a company's image.

Targeting a Demographic: In today's cutthroat marketing environment, studying demographics to make inferences and attract a target group is necessary. Marketing research specialists use analytical tools to harness the power of target demographics to produce effective email marketing campaigns, content marketing initiatives, and a set of actions that allow businesses to provide customers with a personalised experience. To examine which group is most likely to acquire your product or service, or has a need for it, consider the following aspects:

- Age.
- Location.
- Gender.
- Income level.
- Education level.
- Marital or family status.
- Occupation.
- Ethnic background.

5.3.1.3 Competing Aggressively

Competitive aggressiveness entails gaining a brief competitive edge by launching new items, price cuts, and marketing campaigns, among others to provide higher value to customers while confusing competitors. It is a strategy that works for some companies but not for others in newly established marketplaces or highly dynamic sectors. Retailers that succeed with this technique have either specialist technological resources or a large network of dependable partners.

5.3.2 Finding Competitive Prices

The foundational step of any competitive price analysis begins with the collecting of competitive prices. Given the sheer volume of the competitive prices in each location, it is often difficult for retailers to have a complete understanding of the competitive prices at any given point in time. Retailers should use analytics to determine the most important items in each market and the competitor against whom they would be competing with. Once this is done, there are various mechanisms that can be deployed at different frequencies to store and utilise the competitive price data for further analysis and actions.

5.3.2.1 Competitive Price Shop Mechanisms

Retailers have various mechanisms available at their disposal to find competitive prices from the market. These options may be selected based on the fit in a particular market and competitor. For example prices from a competitor who sells its products at the same price online and the stores can be obtained through the process of Web Scraping. In other cases, such as to find prices from a competitor who has no online presence, a comp shop team might have to be engaged. These options along with some other options available are explained below:

5.3.2.2 Web Scraping and Online Pricing

Price scraping is the practice of using web scrapers, which is the extraction of data from a website, to harvest a rival's price data from internet resources, either with or without permission. Price scraping is a technique used by businesses that use dynamic pricing models in different online businesses, such as travel, retail, and e-commerce, to alter their prices and draw customers from competitors. However, to protect their businesses, some e-commerce and travel websites put up hurdles to prevent web scraping.

5.3.2.3 Spy Teams and Comp Shops

Spy team refers to professionals a retailer might use the services of to find the prices followed by competitors. This is done directly or through third-party companies.

In a nutshell, the goal of such professionals/teams is to obtain information on one or more competitors. It comprises gathering private or operational information, such as customer databases, pricing, sales, marketing, R&D, policies, potential bids, planning or marketing strategies, or changing production compositions and locations.

In recent years, it is common to see cell phones beings used to gain knowledge of competitive prices. There are companies that deploy students and people looking for extra income to gather competitive information and get automatically paid for the number of pictures or prices they gather from the market. By using applications and portals, the software is able to automatically add the location and time of the data capture for further analysis.

5.3.2.4 AI and Image Recognition

Artificial Intelligence (AI)-powered solutions can harvest data from millions of web pages in order to uncover useful business insights. These technologies can follow a competitor's whole digital presence, including both on and off their websites. The most important upgrades are not published in a press release but rather hidden in websites or consumer reviews. Web scrapers can dig out these hidden jewels and supply high-quality data.

By recording just a few photographs of retail shelves, in-store automation combined with image recognition allows retail stakeholders to receive real-time visibility into their businesses! At any given time, retail stakeholders can track every stock-keeping unit (SKU) on a shelf across thousands of outlets in any geo-location and time zone.

5.3.2.5 Pricing Business Intelligence and Alerting Mechanism

Price intelligence or competitive price monitoring involves the use of current data mining tools to gain awareness of market-level pricing. These services may be provided by companies that specialise in gathering and providing data to paid subscribers. Further, these service providers might also be able to provide additional insights and analysis based on the competitive prices.

5.3.2.6 Real-Time Monitoring

Automated rival price tracking systems are being increasingly used by retailers. While manual efforts to obtain competitive intelligence become unsalable and unproductive after a certain point, automated pricing mon-itoring solutions do not. These systems require less time to track competitor prices. Leaving more time for the company to focus on the overall strategy and pricing.

Furthermore, internet businesses are working in an increasingly competitive environment that necessitates a proactive response to market shifts on a daily basis. It is hard to provide this critical information without using publicly available real-time data to inform your selections. Today, 94% of customers compare costs before making an online purchase. It is easier for customers to search on competing brands' and merchants' websites to make purchases at a suitable price. This makes competitive pricing an extremely vital feature for brands to attract customers. With dynamic pricing becoming more common, the ability to swiftly react to market fluctuations is becoming a valuable and sought-after competitive advantage. Real-time data equals real-time pricing, ensuring that your company remains competitive. Manually tracking millions of products on the internet is hard, but automated tools can help base pricing strategies on a daily basis.

5.3.2.7 Frequency of Competitive Shopping

Once the mechanism for competitive pricing is determined, the next step is to determine the frequency of the competitive prices based on the intensity and the importance of the competitive price by product-competitor-location. It is important to note that not all products need to be shopped for competitive prices at the same frequency. While some products such as milk and eggs, for example, can be shopped very frequently, such as once a week or day. Some other products such as shampoos and conditioners might be shopped once a month. The most important competitor (perhaps in the most significant competitive market) may be shopped more frequently while a general overview of a larger pool of competitors might be addressed once in 6 months.

5.3.2.8 Data Availability

Data gathered from the competition usually have a short shelf life for a retailer. Sometimes the competitive prices may indicate that a quick reaction is needed either through a change in the retailer's prices or a negotiation with a vendor that can result in higher margins. So it is important to make sure that the gathered data is made available as quickly as possible.

In many cases, the data from the competition is not accurate. Sometimes, there might be an extra or missing digit in the price, the prices might be associated with a different product or model type or the prices captured might be reflecting a promoted price and not an everyday price. This data needs to be cleaned up both through algorithms and human review before usage to avoid making incorrect conclusions.

Furthermore, the collected competitive data needs to be connected to the existing data infrastructure so that the prices gathered can be mapped to the right product location.

5.3.3 Setting Your Price

The process of determining the price for retailers based on the competition can be handled in one of two ways. One, during the initial pricing or optimisation phase and two, in the weekly or periodic price maintenance phase.

During Price optimisation, the competitive strategy determined in the form of CPI goals and product-location level rules forms some of the constraints for the overall optimisation.

Some examples of this include:

- Maintain a CPI index below 95 against Competitor A for "Image Items" in Zone C.
- The overall CPI Index for the category should be below 115 for all Class A Competitors.

- Each product in the product group "KPI -A List" should be at least 10% below its corresponding competitive price with Competitor B.

It is important to note that in some cases the competitive rule might not be met, or be broken to accommodate other higher-priority rules such as a minimum margin rule or a line pricing rule.

With the ongoing price maintenance, new costs and current competitive prices come into play in a dynamic fashion. In this case, the retailers should have pre-determined competitive rules that will help the retailers determine a new competitive price to suit the new market conditions.

It is interesting to note that certain online retail giants have the capability to match competitive prices instantly and automatically. On average, one of the online retail giants changes its price on each product every ten minutes.

Retailers can utilise electronic shelf label (ESL) technology to show the current product pricing on shelves. When the pricing system generates a new price, it automatically updates the price on a shelf. Pricing and promotions are moved to the shelf in real-time, without the need for human intervention or label printing. Through a series of clever procedures, retailers can experiment, sync with the internet, and match the competition.

A quick price-matching strategy is a great method to stay competitive. When driven by rules and algorithms, these prices can move quickly with regard to the market conditions often allowing brick-and-mortar retailers to stay competitive in categories where E-Commerce retail is a direct competition.

5.3.4 Competitive Reactions

While changing prices is one of the techniques retailers can and should use to compete with retailers. It is important to note some of the other techniques retailers can use to compete in the marketplace (Figure 5.4).

Reviewing Competitive Pricing: This helps in avoiding price matching. Following are some queries, retailers can seek answers to:

- Whether the price adjustment for a retailer is temporary or permanent.
- Does the pricing reflect changes in the product or service?
- Whether the pricing adjustment is available to all customers in all the markets or is it limited to a subset.
- How the competitor reacts to the price adjustment and what is the process being followed?
- How much will the pricing adjustment affect the capacity to compete?

Estimating Pricing Effects: All the market data is analysed. The purpose is to gauge the sensitivity of the market to the price adjustment. The customer's price sensitivity is analysed to identify the extent of the impact a price adjustment has had.

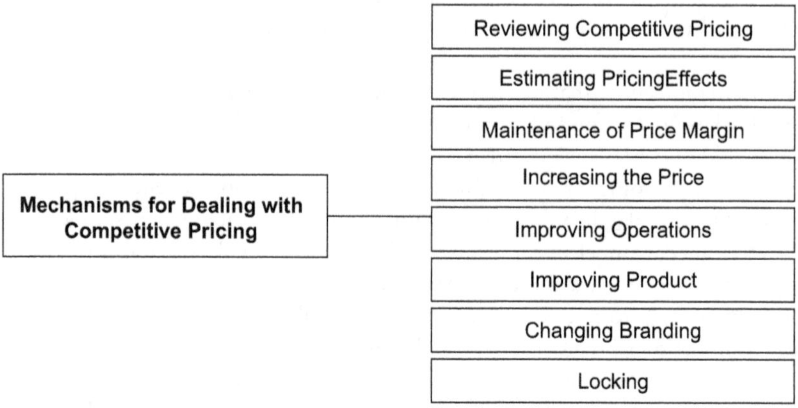

	Reviewing Competitive Pricing
	Estimating PricingEffects
	Maintenance of Price Margin
Mechanisms for Dealing with Competitive Pricing	Increasing the Price
	Improving Operations
	Improving Product
	Changing Branding
	Locking

Figure 5.4 Mechanisms for Dealing with Competitive Pricing.

Maintenance of Price Margin: Retailers need to know that lowering a price will cause losses and loss of market share. However, there is a high chance that the competitor will gain an advantage and the retailer will lose more market share than planned.

Increasing the Price: It is advisable for retailers to increase prices only when making an improvement in quality or when releasing a new product.

Improving Operations: To keep up with the competition, retailers are often forced to make radical changes within the company to survive. This often enhances the company's ability to diversify its goods, and product lines, make innovations and improve distribution channels. To dislodge or match its competitors, a company may even need to acquire a technological breakthrough.

Improving Product: When retailers set pricing that is the same as the competitor's, the differentiating characteristics vanish. The attention moves to the product itself, in this case, the retailer might choose to add or highlight features of the product that are important for the customer.

Changing Branding: To avoid getting compared to similar products by consumers, retailers often use this technique to remain in the competition. They differentiate similar items based on a different brand name, model number, and brand number, among others. For example, if two companies make laundry detergent, both brands would aim to maintain their pricing competitively and market their product to stand out in quality and features in order to compete with the other brand.

Locking: It is a strategy in which retailers are able to make consumers depend on a vendor for products and services that they cannot switch vendors without incurring significant actual or perceived switching costs. Retailers can do so by increasing switching costs or the changes required to be made to switch to another product. Retailers can provide good reasons for consumers to stick, such as by providing a better brand experience or incentives. For example, on Monday, a coffee firm releases a video of its coffee-making process, and on Tuesday, it announces a new coffee flavour and invites consumers to sample it at one of its locations. On Friday, the firm will communicate with customers online to learn about their reactions to the new product.

5.4 Post-markdown Processes and Regulations

Once a competitive strategy and process are set into play, it is important to measure the progress and make corrections with everyday operations. Further, this section also discusses the various regulations and strategic considerations that a retailer needs to be aware of.

5.4.1 Competitive Price Index (CPI)

The Competitive Price Index (CPI) is a measure of the ratio of a retailer's price to the price of its competitors. Through a regular established process, retailers should shop for the competitor's prices and compute the CPIs as KPIs that can be measured continuously.

One way of calculating the CPI is as follows:

$$CPI = \text{Our Price/Competitor's Price}$$
$$\text{Example CPI} = 0.95 = \$9.50/\$10.00$$

Other retailers, use CPIs with the inverse relationship as follows:

$$CPI = \text{Competitor's Price/Our Price}$$
$$\text{Example CPI} = 1.052 = \$10.0/\$9.50$$

CPIs, should be calculated and tracked along the following dimensions:

- By Product Group such as Image Items, Profit Drivers, Etc.
- By competitor.
- By competitor and market combinations.
- Over time dimension.
- By brand, categories and vendors.

5.4.2 Competitive Pricing Regulations

The EU has strict rules in place to protect free competition. Certain practices are prohibited by these rules. If retailers violate the EU's competition rules, they could face a fine of up to 10% of their annual global turnover. Individual managers of offending firms may face serious penalties, including prison, in some

EU countries. EU competition rules apply directly in all EU countries, and your country's courts will enforce them. These rules apply to all organisations engaged in economic activity, not just businesses (such as trade associations, industry groupings, etc).

The competition law used within the European Union is known as European competition law. It promotes the preservation of competition within the European Single Market by regulating anti-competitive behaviour by companies in order to prevent the formation of cartels and monopolies that would harm society's interests. Today's European competition law is primarily derived from articles 101 to 109 of the Treaty on the Functioning of the European Union (TFEU), as well as a number of Regulations and Directives. The following are the four major policy areas:

- Article 101 TFEU defines cartels as the control of collusion and other anti-competitive practices.
- Market dominance, or the prevention of firms abusing dominant market positions under Article 102 TFEU.
- According to European Union merger law, mergers, and control of proposed mergers, acquisitions, and joint ventures involving companies with a certain, defined amount of turnover in the EU.
- Control of direct and indirect aid given to companies by European Union Member States under TFEU article 107.

5.4.3 Vendor Negotiation

A competitor might choose to drop the price of certain products for many of their own internal analyses and reasons. While it might be possible that the competitor has chosen to have a very thin margin to be able to afford selling at a lower price, a very low price can also be the result of a very low cost the competitor has received from their vendors. This scenario becomes especially true if a competitor is able to sell a product at a price below the costs of another retailer. Since most retailers do not or legally cannot sell products at a price below their own costs (unless it is deemed as a markdown or clearance), the lower price indicates that the competitor is receiving a lower cost when compared to the retailer with a higher cost and price. This can form the basis for negotiations with the vendors to allow for fair costs for all. Furthermore, this can be set up in the form of alerts to the category managers to see if a price at a competitor ever falls below our own cost.

5.4.4 Avoiding the Downward Price Spiral

While being competitive is necessary for a retailer's survival and good for the market. Retailers have to be cognizant of the fact that the real goal is to provide value to the customer while still making a healthy profit. Oftentimes, retailers might take a price war as a competition against each other and drop the price until nobody is making a margin and the customer is left with a surplus. If the margins for a particular product are already below a certain threshold, other competitive strategies should be looked into instead of further reducing the price.

5.4.5 Collaborating vs Colluding

Collaboration between competitors is the new mantra for success today. General Motors and Toyota manufacture automobiles, Siemens and Philips develop semiconductors, and Canon supplies Kodak with photocopiers. However, the rise of "competitive collaboration" initiatives, such as joint ventures, outsourcing agreements, product licensing, and cooperative research, have given rise to new efficiencies that are resulting in lower overall prices for consumers.

Collusion, on the other hand, is a non-competitive, secret, and sometimes criminal agreement between competitors to undermine market equilibrium. Collusion takes place when individuals or businesses that would usually compete with one another collaborate to gain an unfair market benefit by working collectively. The colluding parties may collectively opt to influence the supply of a good on the market or accept to set a pricing level that allows the partners to maximise their profits at the expense of other competitors.

This is a common arrangement with duopolies. Collusion can manifest itself in a variety of ways depending on the market. In each situation, a group gains an unfair advantage as a whole. One of the most common types of collusion is price fixing. When a limited group of enterprises, referred to as an oligopoly, compete in a particular supply market, price fixing occurs. This small group of enterprises sells the same product and makes an agreement on pricing. Prices may be dropped forcibly to drive out smaller competitors. Or, they may be raised to support the group's interests at the expense of the buyer. Overall, price fixing can remove or diminish competition while simultaneously raising barriers to entry for newcomers.

It is important to note both the legal and moral obligations of a retailer in its operating markets to ensure both its own survival and fairness to its customers.

5.4.6 Finding Your Positioning

Through an evolved and science-based approach to competitive pricing, retailers might arrive at a dynamic equilibrium which can help determine their competitive position in the marketplace. Retailers may discover that their logistics and operating infrastructure do allow them to position themselves as low-priced retailers with perhaps an Everyday Low Price (EDLP) strategy or perhaps they have a well-oiled promotions mechanism to execute promotions from time to time or a High-Low Strategy.

Furthermore, retailers might uncover that they are particularly well placed to have lower prices in a certain category or market while in other cases, they are well known for their quality or customer service that allows them to command a higher price in the market.

While it is a good idea to "drive" or target a particular position in the market. The market itself can dictate the position a retailer needs to take to survive, a position that can be understood by analysing data.

Chapter 6

Business Intelligence

6.1 Introduction

The procedural and technical infrastructure that collects, stores, and analyses the data generated by a company's operations are referred to as business intelligence (BI). Simply put, it refers to the procedural and technical infrastructure that collects, stores, and analyses data produced by a company (according to Investopedia and Tableau). The BI software combines data mining, process analysis, performance benchmarking, and descriptive analytics. Its goal is to help businesses make data-based business decisions that may help generate revenue, improve operational efficiency, and gain a competitive advantage over competitors. This infrastructure analyses a company's data from all aspects and presents it in simple reports, metrics, and trends which gives managers meaningful insights and helps make better decisions, quickly.

To do this, the BI software uses a combination of analytics, data management, and reporting technologies. (Figure 6.1).

6.2 BI Factors

Understanding the retail customer requires the retailers to measure and comprehend the metrics around several important factors. Retailers need to assess the market landscape, which includes the customer base and the competitive landscape to succeed in the market. Let us explore this in detail in the subsequent sections. Figure 6.2 depicts the factors or considerations to be made for BI.

6.2.1 Business Intelligence Strategy

A BI strategy is a road map that helps companies to use data mining and statistics to assess business performance, search for competitive advantages, and assimilate customer feedback.

Here is what needs to be done:

- Access Current BI Environment: Before analysing where a company is headed, establish a baseline. Many departments would be conducting analysis

DOI: 10.4324/9781003382140-7

Figure 6.1 A Typical Business Intelligence Model.

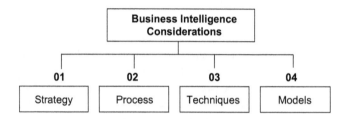

Figure 6.2 Business Intelligence Considerations.

of company or customer data in silos. Like, the marketing team may not have access to sales data or customer service could be tracking user feedback on their own. Worse, there may not be any analytics at all. In short, the company may not have a complete picture. Therefore, the first step would be to get inputs from across the company. This could include the Information Technology (IT) team, department managers, and stakeholders. Then arrange the results to create a SWOT (Strengths, Weaknesses, Opportunities, and Threats) analysis. This important strategy-building tool can help identify the major advantages and challenges for the company.

- Create the Vision: A vision is a mix of direction and purpose. And without a vision, there can be no plan. A vision drives critical decisions, such as where to acquire data and who will have access to the insights. There should be a consensus on who will be in charge of the BI procedures. The next important step would be to establish: the relationship between BI, IT, and company strategy, identify how to provide and support BI solutions, what solutions to adopt and where to implement these, and what infrastructure to build, among others.
- Establish BI Governance: The purpose of BI governance is to define and implement the BI infrastructure. There are three requirements to do this:

  - A BI governance team or individuals in charge of governance procedures
  - BI tools and lifecycle management, and BI architecture design and development.

- User support from a technological, functional, and data viewpoint Create a Roadmap: A roadmap is a visual representation of deliverables at various stages of implementation along with a schedule. The roadmap can simply include high-level activities, such as finding a BI provider or be refined to create a list of the top ten best matches. However, for strategic mappings, a high-level overview will do.
- Create Strategy Document: A strategy document serves as a reference for the whole company and can be used to explain the strategy having the following components:

  - Executive summary
  - Alignment of BI strategy with business strategy
  - Scope and needs of the project
  - BI governance team
  - Alternatives
  - Assessment
  - Appendices

- Review BI Model: Re-evaluation of the BI Maturity model will help evaluate if the company is on the right track. The metrics to review this model are summarised in Figure 6.3. The most important is the return on investment (ROI), which determines if the BI delivered the desired results. It may sometimes be difficult to calculate the ROI for BI projects. The various indirect advantages of deploying a BI system that might be challenging to evaluate are sometimes absent from the direct benefits. Furthermore, there is no universal template that can be used because the indirect advantages for one business may differ from those for another.

6.2.2 Business Intelligence Process

In addition to the BI software, a BI architecture includes smaller data marts that carry subsets of business information for particular departments and business units.

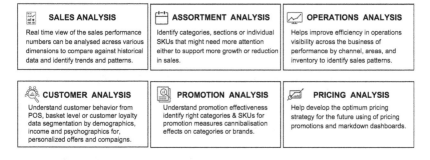

SALES ANALYSIS	ASSORTMENT ANALYSIS	OPERATIONS ANALYSIS
Real time view of the sales performance numbers can be analysed acress various dimensions to compare against historical data and identify trends and patterns.	Identify categories, sections or individual SKUs that might need more attention either to support more growth or reduction in sales.	Helps improve efficiency in operations visibility across the business of performance by channel, areas, and inventory to identify sales patterns.
CUSTOMER ANALYSIS	PROMOTION ANALYSIS	PRICING ANALYSIS
Understand customer behavior from POS, basket level or customer loyalty data segmentation by demographics, income and psychographics for, personalized offers and compaigns.	Understand promotion effectiveness identify right categories & SKUs for promotion measures cannibalisation effects on categories or brands.	Help develop the optimum pricing strategy for the future using of pricing promotions and markdown dashboards.

Figure 6.3 Review of the BI Model.

Invariable, these data marts have links to an enterprise data warehouse where BI data is generally housed. Today, data lakes built on big data platforms are increasingly being used as repositories or landing pads for BI and analytics data, particularly log files, sensor data, text, and other unstructured or semi-structured data.

The BI data can consist of both historical and real-time data acquired simultaneously as it gets generated from source systems. This allows BI tools to support strategic and tactical decision-making. Raw data from various source systems are merged, aggregated, and cleaned using data integration and data quality management technologies before they can be utilised in BI applications. This ensures that BI teams and business users are studying correct data consistently. The following is the general BI process:

- Collecting data, arranging it, and reporting: The data that documents an organisation's everyday transactions serves as the basis for BI. Data may originate from consumer contacts, personnel management, business operations, or financial administration, among other things. The three primary transactional databases used in the conventional approach are CRM (customer relationship management), HRM (human resource management), and ERP (enterprise resource planning). A sales transaction, for instance, would be documented and kept as a piece of data in the CRM database.
- Analysing it to provide knowledge that is useful: To analyse data is to pose questions to it and obtain insightful responses. For instance, the straightforward Excel function "sort in descending order" applied to a column of data indicating sales reps' year-to-date orders would provide the answers to the queries "Who is taking the most orders? What is the least order? The data has been contextualised by the sort command, greatly increasing its significance in light of the business's strategic objectives.
- Making choices that will allow you to achieve your strategic objective: It's interesting to note that the absence of a strategic focus is the main reason why most BI initiatives fail rather than poor technical execution. A corporation should be able to "lift" itself more effectively toward its strategic goals by using BI as a lever. But far too frequently, project managers, CIOs, or CTOs fail to consider BI in the context of the company's objective, leading to it becoming a means in and of itself.

6.2.3 Business Intelligence Techniques

Tools like advanced statistics and techniques like predictive analytics are used by organisations to analyse data, find trends, and forecast outcomes. BI reporting is a continual and complex cycle of data access, investigation, and knowledge exchange. The following are some of the most common BI tools and techniques:

1   Data Mining: This software-based technique throws up patterns and correlations in the (company and customer) data being processed – using databases, statistics, and

machine learning (ML). The extracted data helps in decision-making for developing plans, increasing sales, improving marketing, and more. However, before proceeding with data mining, the following steps need to be followed:

2   Reporting: BI reporting encompasses the entire process of planning, creating performance data, sales data, reconciling data, and preserving content. It supports the management, planning, and decision-making processes by assisting businesses in efficiently gathering and presenting the information. According to their demands, business executives can read the reports every day, every week, or every month.

3   Analytics: Analytics in BI refers to the analysis of data to derive useful conclusions and identify patterns. Business organisations are well known for their use of analytics since it enables analysts and business executives to fully comprehend their data and get value from it. Numerous business facets, including marketing, call centres, and the usage of analytics in various ways. Speech analytics is used in contact centres, for instance, to better convey responses and track consumer sentiment.

4   Data Visualisation: Data is frequently kept in the form of a matrix made up of integers. However, it's a crucial duty to analyse the matrix to make business judgments. When data is saved as a set, anyone, even an analyst, may determine how things are going. The use of data visualisation helps to unravel the tangle. Professionals can look at data from several dimensions using data visualisations to aid in decision-making. As a result, it is simple and practical to grasp the position by visualising the data in charts.

5   OLAP: The key BI method known as online analytical processing (OLAP) is utilised to resolve analytical issues with many dimensions. The flexibility that OLAP's multi-dimensionality affords users to examine data issues from many angles is one of its main advantages. They may even find hidden issues as a result of doing this. To execute activities like budgeting, CRM data analysis, and financial forecasting, OLAP is mostly used.

6   ETL: A special BI method called Extraction-Transaction-Loading (ETL) handles the general data processing procedure. The BI system retrieves data from storage, processes it in the processor, and then loads it. They are mostly employed as transactional tools for transforming data from different sources and storing it in data warehouses. To meet the needs of the business, ETL also modifies the data. By feeding it into end targets like databases or data warehouses, it raises the quality level.

7   Statistical Analysis: Calculations are used in statistical analysis to determine the reliability and significance of observed relationships. With its distribution analysis and confidence intervals, it also understands the behavioural changes in individuals that are evident in the data. After data mining, analysts use statistical analysis to create and get useful solutions.

8   Predictive Modelling: A BI methodology called predictive modelling uses statistical methods to build models that might be applied to trend and

probability forecasts. Using numerous statistical models, predictive modelling enables the prediction of both the value and characteristics of a given data item.

6.2.3.1 Perpetual Licencing

Businesses that prefer to host their data can buy licences for models that are valid for the duration of a program. On-premise implementation requires procurement of hardware, servers, and other infrastructure. It also requires deployment and maintenance of the solution by an IT team. For larger organisations using complex systems or businesses worried about data protection, perpetual licensing may be an appealing option. Such companies may have to pay for licences and infrastructure, maintenance, and product upgrades (many are not always free). Also, the companies need to take in IT labour expenses, vendor support, and the possibility of system failures when calculating their expenditures.

6.2.3.2 Subscription Hosting Plans

Businesses not having or wanting to spend the time or resources to run their solution may explore cloud-based BI software which requires only a monthly or annual subscription fee. The functionality required by such organisations, the types of BI users, and support and maintenance, may also affect subscription prices. Smaller organisations may find cloud-based deployment appealing because it is generally less expensive than an on-premise solution.

The following are the additional costs associated with the BI models:

- Implementation Services: The cost of implementation services varies by vendor. It may include access to a specialised implementation professional, installation, software modification, data migration, database architecture, dashboard template designs, and interaction with other applications, like an Enterprise Resource Planning (ERP) system). Some suppliers have in-house implementation teams while others use external consultants.
- Training Services: Basic training services are provided by some vendors for free while others charge a fee for these, especially if the training is done at the customer location.
- Support Services: Basic support services, such as access to a knowledge base or email, are usually included in the cost. Some suppliers, on the other hand, provide premium support options, such as priority help or access to a personal customer care manager. If retailers choose a perpetual licence, they need to consider that certain suppliers may provide free support and product upgrades for the first year, however, charge additionally for the subsequent years.

6.2.4 Traditional vs Modern Business Intelligence

Traditionally, BI was completely IT-based. That is, requiring the expertise of IT staff alone to create and retrieve data. As a result, reporting and analysis took a top-down approach and decision-makers would have to request analysis or reports from IT professionals only, limiting real-time reporting and with fewer insights. Now, ownership has changed with the evolution of software and ease-of-use functionality. Modern BI is a key business function which is used and owned by almost everyone in the company where easy accessibility is one of the most important features of contemporary BI. Users can engage with data in real time by generating reports and dashboards quickly. The tools, techniques, and technology today enable self-serve analysis. It can be as simple as logging in, viewing dashboards, and generating personalised or customised reports, thanks to analytics that turn data points into consumable insights quickly. Retailers can benefit from modern BI in the following ways:

- Infrastructure: The expense of setting up the infrastructure is one of the most important things to take into account when contrasting the two BIs. The on-premise IT strategy uses traditional BI, or old-school BI, which calls for a significant number of servers, Microsoft SQL licences, and a huge staff of system administrators to develop and manage. This is fantastic if retailers already have everything set up for other technological requirements, but many businesses no longer do so or are unsure of whether they want to go that route. Contrast this with contemporary BI (cloud-based BI), where daily operations may be implemented and managed by only one person. If that doesn't impress, perhaps knowing that the most important interactive reporting for the organisation is accessible 24/7, 365 days a year, and in real-time would. There is no need to wait for irritating static report requests or month-end reports to make judgments. Modern BI is self-service, allowing them to quickly and independently get data from nearly anywhere.
- Availability: One of the main advantages of BI is certainly the accessibility of contemporary BI. Particularly considering that almost all employees have had to work from home at some point since the epidemic struck in 2020, and it appears that many will do so in the years to come. As modern BI is versatile in terms of where and how you may access your BI information, it works well with this new office setup. Everyone has instant access to the same reports and data from any location at any time. This includes at the workplace, when travelling, and using mobile devices and native mobile apps.
- Reliability: Modern BI must be trustworthy to be available, and it is. Even if the workplace loses the internet, BI will continue to function. During a disaster like a hurricane or an earthquake, a company's communication demands increase tenfold, and business choices don't just stop when a network is down because a construction worker outside severed the incorrect

connection. If the workplace lost power or servers crashed, conventional BI would also be unavailable. This would imply that BI is unavailable until that server or power is restored, even if relocated offshore to continue working and had a VPN connection.

- Scalability: The scalability of contemporary BI is astounding. It can expand quickly if necessary and is easily adaptable. Retailers shouldn't compromise this for the company since they need to be flexible to meet its demands if they want to be successful. The contemporary BI can quickly expand with you whether you are a small to a medium-sized organisation with plans for future expansion, both in terms of the number of workers and BI capabilities required. In other words, scaling from 5 to 5000 people is simple and doesn't need the trouble of buying, setting up, and configuring new servers or infrastructure. These are some major differences between traditional and modern (self-serve) BI:
- Easy Accessibility: Traditional BI tools supplied organisations with insights but only through data professionals. This was time-consuming, and restricted accessibility for employees. However, today, everyone can be their data scientist rather than wait for a report to be created, a user may pose queries to any BI tool and receive immediate comprehensive information.
- Cloud Computing and Powerful Analytics: When it comes to managing enormous data and search performance, traditional BI solutions fall short. They were not designed to manage huge amounts of data, particularly across several clouds. Modern BI systems' distributed cluster management allows it to scale with a company's data volume and has high processing speed.
- Artificial Intelligence: Artificial intelligence (AI) bridges the gap between traditional corporate intelligence and current self-serve analytics. Traditional BI solutions provided insights that were either pre-set or manually managed by data experts. We saw this slowed down productivity and reduced the amount of information a company could gather. To extract maximum value from data, current BI and analytics services include AI and ML. The AI engine accomplishes this by analysing billions of rows of data using hundreds of insight-detection algorithms.
- Voice Analytics: The most significant distinction between conventional and current BI services is voice analytics, which, together with AI and ML applications to data, is arguably the most significant feature. Employees that require answers away from their workstations, whether in a retail store or a manufacturing plant, may use this technology to get analysis within seconds.

6.3 Tools of Business Intelligence

Modern BI offers several tools today. See Figure 6.4. Some of the most distinct tools having essential characteristics and functions required by most businesses today are described as follows:

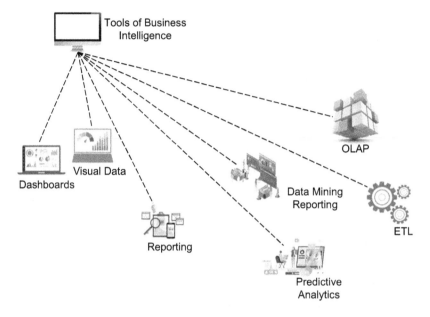

Figure 6.4 Modern Business Intelligence Tools.

• Dashboards: Dashboards are visual data reports providing highlights of the data at a glance. Being dynamic, dashboards are one of the most popular BI tools as they offer simple data analysis, customise information for a company, and allow users to share the researched information with others. Dashboards can have charts, graphs, snapshots, and reports on a single page with interactive features like filters to provide options for different views. Dashboards can be of the following types:

  • Operational: Informs about the current situation
  • Strategic: Tracks key performance indicators (KPIs)
  • Analytical: Processes data to identify the existing trends

• Visual Data: There are several ways to visualise data. Following are some of the most frequently used:

  • Pie charts
  • Bar graphs
  • Histograms
  • Gantt charts
  • Heat maps
  • Box and whisker plots
  • Waterfall charts

- Area graphs
- Scatter plots
- Infographics
- Maps

- Reporting: The goal of reporting is to communicate raw data into useful information as reports. The following are a few reporting tools that are widely used:

  - ActiveReports
  - Actuate Corporation
  - BOARD
  - Business Objects
  - Cognos BI
  - Crystal Reports
  - CyberQuery
  - GoodData
  - MATLAB
  - TIBCO
  - Zoomdata

- Predictive Analytics: Predictive analytics software identifies patterns and best practices in any business by analysing current data. This program may be used by marketing teams to identify new consumer bases to protect their profits, while financial and insurance companies can make risk-assessment. It can be used by manufacturing and retail companies to forecast demand variations or how any process modifications can influence supply networks. Following are a few predictive analytics software:

  - EverString
  - Infer
  - Radius
  - HALO
  - SAS Advanced Analytics
  - IBM SPSS
  - SAP HANA

- Data Mining Reporting: Data mining tools are software applications that can create and test data models by structuring and executing data mining procedures. A few examples are as follows:

  - Rapid Miner
  - Oracle Data Mining
  - IBM SPSS Modeler
  - Knime
  - Python
  - Orange

- Kaggle
- Rattle
- Weka
- Teradata

- Extract Transform and Load (ETL): An ETL tool extracts data from one or more data sources, then transforms and cleans it to make it suitable for reporting and analysis. This new data is then saved in a data store or warehouse. Some examples of ETL are:

  - Informatica PowerCenter
  - IBM InfoSphere DataStage
  - Oracle Data Integrator (ODI)
  - Microsoft SQL Server Integration Services
  - Ab Initio
  - SAP Data Services
  - SAS Data Manager

- Online Analytical Processing (OLAP): This software solution allows users to analyse information from multiple database systems simultaneously. It speeds up analysis to provide unlimited report viewing, complicated analytical computations, and predictive "what if" scenarios (budget, forecast) and planning capabilities. Some examples are:

  - Dundas BI
  - Sisense
  - IBM Cognos Analytics
  - InetSoft
  - SAP Business Intelligence
  - Halo

6.4 Business Intelligence for Pricing

A technology-driven process aids in the translation of raw data into meaningful insights, allowing organisations to make better decisions. It usually entails using analytics to identify trends and patterns, but it can be done in a variety of ways. This is especially useful when it comes to improving customer engagement, which is where real-time data tools come in handy. This allows sales teams to create customer profiles, habits, and potential interest areas. It goes without saying that the more you know about your customers, the better you will be able to connect with them and provide excellent service.

Here are some ways retailers can improve their BI capabilities by utilising various solutions tailored to their specific requirements.

- Visualisation and Dashboards
- Data mining

- Predictive Analytics
- Prescriptive Analytics
- Text Analytics

Using analytics solutions, retail managers, decision-makers, and end-users can create modern BI dashboards to display key data from various departments in a single, cohesive view. This can assist retailers in identifying trends and making more informed operational decisions. Data analytics is essential for developing an effective BI dashboard because it allows businesses to understand how their operations are performing. This can be useful for identifying areas for improvement and tracking progress over time. A BI solution that collects key metrics is especially important in the retail industry because it allows for the monitoring of sales and inventory levels. This can help to keep inventory to a minimum while increasing sales and profits.

6.4.1 Benefits of Business Intelligence for Pricing

Sales are sure to boost and profits jump when companies can extract critical information from operational data and act proactively. The good news is that most companies today can afford the BI solutions required to facilitate this data analysis. To sum up, good BI can help retailers in the following ways:

- Accurate and fast reporting: Employees may monitor KPIs using a range of data sources, including price margin monitoring, promotion performance, and markdown reports.
- Valuable insights: Companies may assess department-specific performance as well as previously defined indices.
- Competitive analysis: The competitive intelligence gathered along with the additional analysis performed on it can be utilised by the category management and pricing teams through a well-designed BI platform.
- Finding market trends: Businesses may get a competitive edge, directly affect long-term profitability, and get a clear picture of what is going on by seeing new possibilities and developing a plan with supporting data. By examining consumer information, and market circumstances, and identifying company issues, employees may use internal data and external market data to identify new sales trends.
- Better, more accurate decisions: Since competitors move swiftly, businesses must reach conclusions as soon as possible. Inaccuracies and delays might cost businesses consumers and revenue. Organisations may make use of available data to optimise time to decision by providing information to the appropriate stakeholders at the appropriate time.
- Increased revenue: Businesses may use data from BI systems to discover sales shortcomings and make comparisons across several dimensions to ask better questions to understand their customer behaviours.

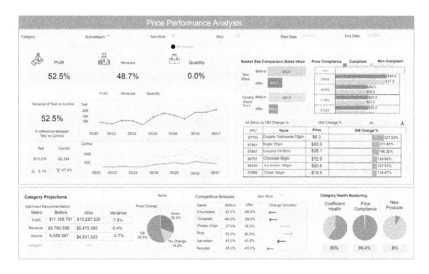

Figure 6.5 A Sample Retail Pricing Dashboard.

• Staying abreast with Cost changes: Retailers can leverage the BI infrastructure to monitor cost changes and to react quickly when the cost of their products changes. Alerts can be set up on the platform for low or negative margins.

Retail Pricing Dashboard: A retail pricing dashboard (such as the one shown in Figure 6.5) may be used to track several components of the results of a pricing process. Some elements of this dashboard are described below:

Key Metrics Tracking: Profit, Revenue, and Units are tracked. When a Test vs Control implementation is set up, these metrics can provide critical information on the performance of the new prices implemented in stores.

Basket Size: It is important to note how the prices being implemented are impacting the basket size of the customers. This can be tracked as a "before" vs "after" of the pricing exercise or with the Test vs Control mechanism as well.

Inventory Turns: The inventory turns for each product or aggregation level is a popular metric retailers use to measure the performance of product sales.

Category Sales: When a product is promoted or is being sold at a new price, it might be a good idea to measure the product's performance when compared to the sales of the entire category or subcategory to which the product belongs to.

Top/Bottom Performers: At a glance, identifying the most profitable and least profitable (or loss-making) products can enable retailers to make quick actions as need be.

Competitive Price Indices (CPIs): As discussed in the chapter on Competition, several CPI indices can be tracked to ensure the prices are in line with the competitive environment.

Promotional Performance: As discussed in the chapter on Promotions, several promotion performance charts and metrics can be tracked to ensure the promoted prices are performing as expected.

Price Compliance: Often a well-intentioned price determined after careful consideration might not get implemented in the retail storefront due to logistics issues. A price compliance dashboard can quickly point this gap to the decision-makers so that appropriate corrective action might be taken.

Category Health Monitoring: The overall health of the prices which are live in the store can be measured mathematically. This can be based on the number of prices being at their "optimal price", the number of new products in the assortment which have no coefficients assigned to them and the actual performance of the modelling coefficients which have been already used to make the calculations. This health index can be leveraged to determine the need for remodelling or reoptimisation of the category.

6.5 Business Intelligence Future Trends

Today, BI has become a valuable tool for both large and small businesses. It has seen several transformations in the last two decades and many more trends are anticipated in the coming years as all companies want to use the technology. Figure 6.6 depicts this ongoing transformation – from offering simple functions to more complex and diverse uses.

- AI-Based Predictive Business Analytics: Businesses rely on analytical tools that can predict the outcomes of a company's strategies and goals. However, over time as businesses and their data grow, companies cannot work with old technologies. High-end AI technologies that conduct predictive analysis with high efficiency are increasingly being used.
- Self-Service BI Solutions: BI solutions have relied on data storage in central warehouses. However, as organisations have grown in size and the requirement of numerous users to access large amounts of data in a short period of time has increased. As a result, businesses are increasingly turning to self-service business

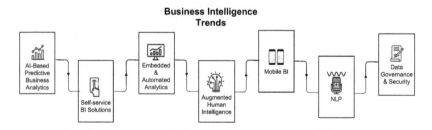

Figure 6.6 BI Future Trends Expected in the Retail Industry.

information, which offers information to several users causing less dependence on data professionals.

- Embedded and Automated Analytics: The number of data sources available today has grown dramatically but an organisation's capacity to collect and evaluate all the information is still limited. The much-needed data automation in BI is projected to increase dramatically, thereby allowing dealing with even bigger data sets in the coming years. Embedded analytics is being used by both large and small organisations. Thus, BI will be integrated with native apps and made available through dashboards which will increase the speed with which data is analysed, allowing businesses to make faster decisions. Also, embedded analytics will reduce the need to switch between different tools.

- Augmented Human Intelligence: The relevance of this breakthrough has been recognised by the corporate sector. Augmented analytics is anticipated to get a lot more attention in the near future. It integrates human intellect and provides contextual awareness via AI, paving the way for ML-based automation. Experts who can work on new data management technologies will be needed by companies. AI-assisted tools will ensure that employees with rudimentary computer science understanding will be able to execute various programs.

- Mobile BI: The fundamental goal of BI is to ensure all users can access data and make informed decisions based on statistics. BI in more forms will be accessible on mobile devices. This way, personnel in faraway locations will be able to access real-time data and set up alerts, notifications, and other tools to improve operations.

- Natural Language Processing (NLP): NLP is a form of AI that allows machines to read and interpret human language. The advancement of NLP has significantly enhanced how businesses acquire and extract useful data. There are some instances of NLP that BI applications will increasingly rely on in the future, such as natural language generation, speech recognition, ML, and teaching.

- Data Governance and Security: Data governance covers data management policies, technology, and employees. Customers have become aware of how companies manage their personal information and are concerned about data breaches. They now expect more transparent data management and security practices. Businesses, large or small, need to take data privacy policy and execution seriously. Moreover, the General Data Protection Regulation ("Regulation") and the Data Protection Directive for the police and criminal justice sector are parts of the data protection reform package that went into effect in May 2016 and is effective as of May 2018 (IP/17/386). The reform is crucial for bolstering people's basic rights in the digital age and promoting commerce by streamlining regulations for businesses operating in the Digital Single Market. The General Data Protection Regulation is the cornerstone of the Digital Single Market's open data exchange. The Commission wants to make sure that everyone is prepared for its implementation on 25 May 2018, including EU governments, national data protection agencies, businesses, and individuals. The legislation was passed in April 2016. Although the rule is immediately applicable, several things still need to be changed significantly for it to function effectively in practice. Examples include modifying current laws by EU governments or creating the European Data Protection Board data protection authorities.

Chapter 7

E-Commerce Pricing

7.1 Introduction

A well-conceived e-commerce pricing strategy entails appropriate pricing of products and services – to boost sales and profits while remaining competitive. Depending on the type of goods offered, demand for products, and prevailing competition, there are several e-commerce pricing techniques used today.

Pricing in e-commerce or online companies is complex as the competition is getting tougher. As we know, manufacturers propose a manufacturer's suggested retail price (MSRP), also known as the list price or the recommended retail price or the suggested retail price of a product. It is the price at which its manufacturer recommends a retailer to sell that product. Now, a dealer may choose to sell it at that price, or sell it above or below that price. However, as online merchants offer frequent and higher, discounts, and special offers, the MSRP has less clout online.

7.2 E-Commerce Pricing Considerations

Retailers do not want to undervalue their products or services and their brand. However, retailers also do not want to price themselves out of the market. So how do retailers determine whether their price is appropriate?

Figure 7.1 depicts the five main factors for new and established e-commerce companies to consider while pricing their products and services. These main considerations are described in the following sections:

7.2.1 Maintaining Transparency

Customers today are spoilt for choice when it comes to shopping online. However, for customers even today, transparency in doing transactions is of utmost importance. So much so that it impacts their choice of website. Customers want e-commerce companies to be open and honest with them, especially with the billing. Therefore, transparency is advantageous not only to

DOI: 10.4324/9781003382140-8

Figure 7.1 E-Commerce Pricing Considerations.

customers but also to businesses. Customers are happier and there are fewer abandoned shopping carts on the site when there is more transparency.

Pricing is critical for enhancing transparency. Customers do not want to be taken by surprise during the checkout process by unexpected or hidden charges associated with the products being purchased. For example, if the price of a product a customer is contemplating buying is dependent on the number of items purchased, the customer would like that to be made explicit before the person can add the product to the cart.

7.2.2 Omnichannel Pricing

Omnichannel pricing refers to an approach by a retailer to provide customers with uniform pricing that is reflected across all its customer channels.

This helps retailers enhance the customer experience. Omnichannel pricing is the way to go for retailers to retain customers in today's competitive market. Customers need not browse a competitor's website before making a purchase.

Argos, a catalogue retailer located in the United Kingdom, allows customers to order online and then pick it up in a store. The business ensures that the prices displayed online are the same as what the customer pays in the store. The option of buying online and picking up in-store or opting for home delivery, puts the power in the hands of the customers, allowing them to make a choice.

7.2.3 Customer Data

Customer data is collected both in stores and online by businesses for many reasons. Collecting customer data allows a business to gain further insights into customer behaviour and preferences. The business can then use this information to not just retain the customer but expand the customer base. In a nutshell, it benefits both the company and the customer.

Online stores can acquire information from customers in several ways. However, e-commerce businesses need to obtain this information responsibly. Here are some ways to gather customer information:

- Offer Incentives: Customers who give their information can be offered a discount by a business.
- Explain the Benefits: Invite the customer to participate in surveys (a questionnaire that a retail company delivers to its consumers) to receive more personalised recommendations for shopping and other offers. If customers know the surveys will benefit them, they are more likely to participate.
- Flexibility in Email Subscriptions: Allow users to opt out of email subscriptions and give them control over the information they want to receive. This makes a customer feel secure.

Gathering customer information helps companies in many ways. To better serve consumers' requirements and increase sales, retailers might utilise this data to customise their purchasing, marketing, and price decisions. For starters, it helps businesses provide shoppers with a more tailored shopping experience by learning about their preferences. Moreover, businesses can learn from past misses and improve their operations to delight customers. Let's see the benefits of customer data gathering:

- Better market understanding: The ability to get a deeper knowledge of how customers act online, define general demographics, and pinpoint opportunities to enhance the customer experience is perhaps the main reason why so many businesses gather consumer data. Data makes it far simpler for businesses to comprehend what clients desire, the particular goods or services they're hunting for, and even how they like to communicate with the brand. Moreover, knowing more about clients will allow modifying every aspect of the company to better suit their requirements. Additionally, retailers may enhance the channels through which they can speak with the target audience, optimise the website to enhance user experience, etc.
- Improves customer database: The collection of consumer data may undoubtedly aid in achieving the goal of expanding and organising the company database, which we know retailers are always striving to do. The IP addresses, email addresses, and perhaps even phone numbers of those who have engaged with the brand in some manner will be available for collection. As a result, retailers may get in touch with them about potential future possibilities, enhance lead generation approach, and more accurately determine the degree of interest a customer has in the business based on how they behave on the website or react to adverts in other ways. Thus, retailers invest more time, effort, and marketing dollars into generating quality leads. Retailers will be

able to send those SMS marketing updates, email newsletters, exclusive deals, etc.

- Improve marketing strategies: Company's total digital marketing strategy is more crucial than ever, especially in the modern world. Retailers must make every effort to improve their marketing strategy if retailers want to rank higher than their rivals, enhance conversions, and build a relationship of transparency and trust with their market. The fact of the matter is that retailers simply cannot accomplish this without gathering data and utilising it to guide every aspect of how they promote goods and services to consumers. To make future commercials more successful and specifically targeted, data will be able to inform which of the marketing campaigns and strategies the target audience responds to and favours. The average customer profile, their favourite social networking sites, the things they are most interested in, and much more will be revealed to retailers. Additionally, data can assist in gaining a deeper understanding of the general client path/journey on the website. By doing so, retailers may implement the required adjustments to enhance user experience and encourage conversion.

- Greater personalisation: When it comes to marketing and product recommendations, purchase confirmations, and any other type of contact between them and the company, over 63% of customers say they want customisation from the businesses they do business with. Retailers may fulfil customer expectations for individualised messages and recommendations by collecting data. Furthermore, retailers are more likely to seal the sale by pitching them the goods and services they are most likely to purchase if retailers have a better understanding of the kind of goods and services they are interested in. Retailers may group consumers with similar interests together in marketing segments, enable autocompletion of payment information and other fields on online forms, and even learn more about the devices that people use to visit websites. This significantly enhances ROI, reduces the sales cycle, and paves the door for the type of expansion retailers have always envisioned.

Note that there are some challenges in gathering customer data. Customers are wary about disclosing personal information and this can make collecting data difficult. Companies need to reassure customers that their information is safe with them and will not be misused.

Retailers should ensure that the collected customer data complies with the various data privacy requirements that apply to the region.

7.2.4 Customer Shopping Behaviour

Behavioural pricing is a relatively recent concept in commodity pricing. The behaviour of potential buyers is used to determine product pricing. The browser search history, click patterns during online purchasing, demographic data, and profiles on social networks can all be used to determine behaviour patterns. Pricing based on client behaviour includes psychological, emotional, and behavioural factors.

Note that behavioural pricing is meant to supplement rather than replace the traditional pricing strategy. It seeks to identify the following:

- How do customers interpret and handle price information?
- What are their reactions to pricing quotations?
- How do customers make decisions and judgements based on given price information?

A stimulus-response system that explains the customer's actions serves as the foundation for these cognitive processes. A stimulus serves as the beginning point. It is perceived by the customer and results in a subjective evaluation. Individual conduct, that is a reaction, is the end consequence.

For example, let us take the case of a customer looking for a winter coat. The person searches on Google and visits several online retailers and merchant platforms. One store employing behavioural pricing tracks the customer's visits. The merchant reads the related data, such as the browser's search history or the website's breadcrumbs. Now suppose the customer initially leaves the site but returns 2 weeks later to look at the product page. The store notes that the customer is interested in that product as this is the second visit. The shop may use this information to raise the winter coat. This does happen in practice. When customers return to certain stores and product pages multiple times, the prices of products are slightly altered, in fact often, increased, by say 5% every time. This may be perceived by the customer as a signal to act. The customer often believes the price will continue to grow. Therefore, makes a purchase.

7.2.5 Real-Time Store Monitoring

Real-time store monitoring involves the use of technologies of several types to help monitor almost all store activity continually during working hours. It provides analytical data on a store's performance. These platforms are used especially by multichannel retailers for managing data on inventory, sales, and customer behaviour. This monitoring also helps identify customers who are critical to a company's success. Retailers strive to improve their customers' shopping conveniences. Knowing customer preferences and purchase patterns is becoming increasingly crucial in a highly competitive industry like retail. In traditional in-store retailing, both customers (real-time and traditional) are found to be identical, in contrast to the customised purchasing online experiences. Retail in-store control (regulates the flow of communication with retail stores via any internet-connected device to productively and efficiently converge visual merchandising criteria) is a crucial approach to creating a healthier store experience. It assists retailers in gaining valuable insights into customer behaviour – by analysing customer feedback, purchasing patterns, and demographic variables.

These stores are now utilising technology such as machine intelligence (ML) and deep learning to provide high levels of customer service. This monitoring even allows stores to go without cashiers, which means customers can skip the checkout queues. The systems can track the products purchased, do the billing automatically, and enables billing through apps – while also providing customer data.

For example, Amazon Go has retail stores where customers need to download their app for entry. Thereafter, they can shop and select products in the store. Billing is done in real-time. After completing the shopping, the billing information is mailed to the customer.

7.3 E-Commerce Pricing Strategy

Online companies need a well-executed e-commerce pricing strategy to price items appropriately to not just boost sales but also stay competitive. Needless to say customer loyalty to a product and/or brand is at the heart of the e-commerce pricing strategy. Depending on the type of goods offered, the demand for products, and ensuing competition, several types of e-commerce pricing techniques have evolved and are employed.

Each company's optimal e-commerce pricing approach is unique. Moreover, it needs to change as a company grows. For example, a basic cost-plus pricing approach focuses on making a profit from each transaction and is effective in the early phases of a company. However, it may not be viable as the company establishes itself. Or if a company's costs shoot up, the real cost per order (CPO) and/or customer acquisition cost (CAC) may rise as well.

7.3.1 E-Commerce Pricing Strategies

Even a profitable e-commerce business may be able to increase earnings if it keeps improving its pricing approach. Figure 7.2 displays some pricing strategies followed by many big retail companies. Let us look at these more closely:

1   Cost-Plus Pricing: To arrive at a selling price, the cost-plus pricing approach entails adding a certain percentage amount to the cost of products and services. To calculate a product's pricing, the material cost, labour cost, and

Figure 7.2 E-Commerce Pricing Strategies.

overhead expenses are combined, and then a markup percentage is added. In a customer contract, cost-plus pricing can also be employed.

2 Competition-Based Pricing: In the competition-based pricing technique, a business determines the price of its items after studying the competition. This method does not include the beginning expenditures or start-up costs and solely considers the selling price of competitors.

3 Value-Based Pricing: Value-based pricing is a pricing approach that is based on a customer's perception of a product's or service's value. It is also referred to as customer-based pricing.

4 Loss-Leader Pricing: This type of pricing focuses on selling products at a loss to persuade people to buy a more expensive product. Customers purchase related products required to make the offered product effective, which helps to cover the cost of the loss. For example, a printer and printer ink, a video console and a video game, among others. The additional items can be acquired at the time of the first sale or at a later time. Razor and blades are an example of a product that employs loss-leader pricing. Most razors come with a cartridge of blades and are reasonably priced. However, when it is time to replace the blades a customer may find that the blades are expensive. Yet, they will pay for more blades because they already own a razor. Loss-leader pricing may be used to boost average order value by enticing customers to buy the complimentary product – in addition to the low-cost product. Thus, making them add more to their cart as they perceive they are getting a good bargain.

5 Price Skimming: Price skimming, often referred to as skim pricing, is a pricing tactic where a business charges a high beginning price before progressively lowering it to appeal to increasingly price-sensitive clients. When there is little to no competition, a first mover typically employs the price approach. Price skimming is not a long-term price strategy that will work since competing companies will ultimately release their items and put pressure on the initial company's pricing.

6 Dynamic Pricing: Dynamic pricing, also known as surge pricing, demand pricing, or time-based pricing, is a pricing technique in which retailers establish variable prices for products or services based on market demand. Retailers can adjust their rates based on algorithms that consider competition pricing, supply and demand, and other market external variables.

7 Premium Pricing: This marketing technique entails strategically pricing a retailer's goods more than the direct competitors. The goal of premium pricing is to create a perception in the market that the retailer's product is just a little bit better than the competition. It is most effective when combined with a well-coordinated marketing campaign aimed at improving that perception. The price skimming technique is strongly linked to premium pricing. In contrast to skimming, it entails setting high rates and maintaining them. Luxury brands have long used premium pricing though it is also used in software as a service (SaaS).

8   Anchor Pricing: This technique of setting a price point that customers may refer
     to while making decisions is known as price anchoring. When you see a discount
     written as, say, $100 $75, it means $100 is the price anchor for the $75 sales price.

7.3.1.1 Combining Strategies

If it makes sense for a retailer, the retailer can mix e-commerce pricing techniques during certain periods. Dynamic pricing in combination with
competitor-based pricing can assist a retailer in remaining competitive.

In the long term, combining loss-leader pricing with price skimming can
boost customer loyalty, trust, and value since customers will continue to buy
products from the same retailer as prices drop.

To justify high pricing, a retailer might mix value-cost and competitive-based
pricing. Thus, by convincing buyers to purchase the expensive items that are
worth the extra cost, a retailer may demonstrate that they offer unique features,
superior materials, and damage resistance, among others.

7.3.2 Optimisation of E-Commerce Pricing

For online firms, maintaining high levels of growth requires price optimisation.
We don't live in a static world, thus it is crucial. Our world is continuously
changing and in motion. Consumers' requirements, wants, tastes, and finances
are always shifting. What's "hot" varies and develops over time in various
consumer marketplaces. Regulations, trade policies, and tax policies all constantly alter your expenses. Pricing optimisation is the process of determining the
product's best-performing, most ideal price. Higher conversion rates and client
lifetime values are required to balance off the increased competition in digital
advertising and rising customer acquisition expenses. The majority of businesses
make changes too late to have an impact. This is why e-commerce firms must
have the tools they need to keep track of how the world is changing and
implement the appropriate price changes to enable year-over-year growth by
lowering customer acquisition costs and raising customer value. The secret is
being able to spot trends in the shifting environment as they emerge so that you
can take full advantage of them. To optimise established pricing, companies can
further employ software-based technologies as shown in Figure 7.3.

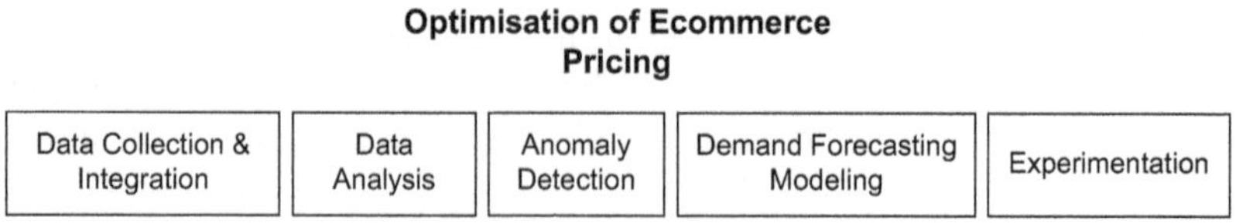

Optimisation of Ecommerce Pricing

Data Collection & Integration	Data Analysis	Anomaly Detection	Demand Forecasting Modeling	Experimentation

Figure 7.3 Optimisation of E-Commerce Pricing.

1 Data Collection and Integration: The first step is to create a data set using the available sources of data to create the demand forecasting models. The sales dataset having the sales information for the retailer is the basis to begin working on any pricing optimisation project. Whether the retailer is an e-commerce or brick-and-mortar retailer, the research begins with the sales data.

Typically, businesses will structure their sales data on one of the following basis:

- By Sales Transactions: Each transaction's item identifier, date, number of goods sold, and sale price are all listed. The payment method (cash, credit card, etc.) and shipment details might be beneficial in supplementing this information.
- By Daily Aggregation: Some retailers do this to keep track of their sales data since they need to keep track of their cash flow.

   Now sales data is just one of many aspects to consider. As demand is influenced by many factors including price, competitor's pricing, season, holidays, and macroeconomic conditions.

   Other data examined can be as follows:

- Category, sub-category, description, number of photographs, photos, and general characteristics are used to profile each item and compare it with others.
- Different metrics such as Gross Domestic Product (GDP), unemployment rate, consumer confidence, and currency exchange make up macro-economics. Note that these indications were obtained during different periods. Some are computed quarterly, some monthly, and others daily.
- Information about stores or sellers, such as location, size, and so on.
- Holidays and events: Some holidays and events, such as Valentine's Day, Christmas, and Mother's Day can have a direct influence on the number of sales of certain goods.
- Other customers' reviews can also be incorporated into the predicting model.
- The presence of one or more significant competitors might have a direct influence on the demand for goods. Knowing their prices may provide significant insights.
- Customer traffic includes the number of visits (both online and offline), the average time spent on a page, and the number of clicks for online stores.
- Details about the retailer's background, and type, among others.

2 Data Analysis: After collecting the sales dataset, the data is now ready to be analysed. The retailers now need to identify the products to start optimising. Clean data are given here and are prepared for analysis at this stage. Retailers may make inferences from the data sets that will help in

making more knowledgeable business judgments. Retailers will need artificial intelligence (AI) technologies or personnel at this point to assist in sorting through the data. Data analysis is a popular area of study nowadays, therefore some experts can assist sort it. Once data has been structured for reporting, there are four methods to interpret it:

- Descriptive analysis: It acts as the foundation for BI tools and dashboards. It explains what occurred. It closely examines how frequently it occurred as well as when and where it took place. Applications of descriptive analysis in e-commerce include: KPI dashboards, monthly revenue reports, and an overview of sales leads are the main tools used to show how a firm is performing about selected benchmarks.
- Diagnostic analysis: Through diagnostic analysis, corporate processes are better understood, and the "Why did it happen?" issue is resolved. This kind of analytics aids businesses in drawing precise linkages between data and patterns of behaviour. The applications of diagnostic analysis in e-commerce are to analyse the revenue decline (for instance, if the website displayed noticeably lower revenue last month, the retailer may use a drill-down exercise to remind about a server failure or more days off than usual due to holidays, which helps explain the decline); identifying the marketing initiatives that resulted in a rise in purchase activity or a summary of sales leads.
- Predictive analysis: Predictive analysis examines patterns, dependencies, and cause-and-effect linkages. The issue of "What is likely to happen?" is addressed in this stage. The information narrates your customers' experiences. It is possible to make rational predictions using this knowledge. The predictive analytics applications in e-commerce are risk assessment, sales forecasting, and figuring out which leads are most likely to convert.
- Prescriptive analysis: Prescriptive analysis is the process through which big data and artificial intelligence work together to forecast outcomes in complex situations. This process needs specialised software. It asks, "What is the best course of action in this circumstance?" Will trying something this way result in a better outcome? is another question that may be posed. This kind of analysis offers the best course of action given the situation. The applications of prescriptive analysis in e-commerce are scheduling (delivering the right products at the right time) and customer experience optimisation production line optimisation.

3 Anomaly Detection: This involves detecting anomalies in the data which could be variances, deviations, and outliers from the norm. An anomaly detection report covers four major themes in a typical retail scenario:

- Increase in online purchases: Anomaly detection tools let teams monitor any abrupt changes in the number of completed transactions, such as an unexpected spike in demand, for retail organisations. Numerous factors, such as Christmas shopping and abrupt changes in the weather, might cause demand to increase. For example, the Covid-19 pandemic has increased demand for and thus reduced the availability of N95 masks at the start of the pandemic. Businesses may monitor their inventory levels and make crucial business choices, such as purchasing more supplies or locating substitute items that satisfactorily satisfy their customers' demands, by rapidly recognising spikes in sales.

- Finding expensive bugs: Teams can more easily uncover those difficult-to-find errors, such as a mispriced item or an incorrect tax computation, with the use of anomaly detection software. There is a good likelihood that a product was mispriced or that a colleague unintentionally allowed a promotion to run for an excessively long period if income decreased less than anticipated but conversion rates (particularly the proportion of customers making a buy) remained high. Similar to the previous point, anomaly detection technology aids retail teams in identifying design defects that cause consumer annoyance and produce adverse outcomes, such as rises in the website's bounce rate or unexpected spikes in the rate of shopping cart abandonment.
- Tracking marketing initiatives: Anomaly detection technology may also be used by retailers and e-commerce companies to gauge the success of new promotions or marketing campaigns. The retailer's team is better able to evaluate data and answer important questions such as, "Are we seeing enough individuals converting (making a purchase) to offset discounts?" or "How can we find income potential from coupon errors?" by employing retail-focused anomaly detection approaches.
- Identifying business opportunities: The numerous retail anomaly detection techniques help teams find new business prospects, stop revenue leakage, and gain a better grasp of the demographics of the target customers, including their age, gender, and location. After all, it's important to have a deeper knowledge of the users, particularly their buying habits, to make sure retailers are providing them with the goods and services they both desire and need.

4 Demand Forecasting Modelling: Based on previous sales data, demand forecasting is a procedure used to estimate future consumer demand. Supply chain management and a wide range of other corporate processes are impacted by forecast accuracy. The objective is to be able to construct a demand curve for each product. This will help us understand how demand is affected by factors including pricing, holidays/events, and macroeconomics. Collaboration with the business team is crucial during this period. Business insights assist in validating the chosen characteristics and ensuring that no significant component is overlooked that is required to anticipate demand. Models for demand forecasting are often divided into two categories:

quantitative approaches and qualitative methods. When large data is unavailable, such as when new items are invented and sales data is nonexistent, qualitative approaches might be helpful. Quantitative techniques use technologies like machine learning to analyse massive data and forecast future consumer demand. The following are some qualitative and quantitative approaches to demand forecasting models:

- Trend projection: It uses data from previous sales to make projections about future sales, and is typically thought of as the most straightforward and streamlined forecasting approach possible. Business experts should update their trend estimates in real-time when unexpected and significant changes take place to preserve forecasting accuracy over the long run. An unanticipated change that would need a trend prediction update may be anything as simple as a social media shoutout from a well-known influencer or a supply chain management error.
- Composite sales force: Sales force composite, which projects demand based on feedback from the sales team, offers exclusive information on consumer preferences and rivals. The process of projecting the sales force composite requires close departmental coordination, including managers and supervisors. Business executives need to take into account the fact that the sales force composite approach has a significant amount of human bias. For this reason, the sales force composite forecasting approach is frequently employed in conjunction with quantitative techniques.
- Delphi approach: Surveys and questionnaires are used in the Delphi approach to anticipate future demand. An educated and united agreement among experts is the paradigm of forecasting used by Delphi.
- Market research: For freshly created businesses that need to comprehend client demand patterns but lack access to historical sales data, market research forecasting is suitable. Demand patterns are discovered through the use of consumer feedback surveys, and subsequent marketing campaigns may be tailored to target particular groups. Market research may take place over a short period or be included in an ongoing business operation.
- Econometrics: It is a big data-heavy field that relies on the intricate study of outside variables. Due to the enormous amount of data that has to be analysed, machine learning methods are particularly beneficial for econometrics. Finding correlations between external economic elements is econometrics' main goal. Customers whose salaries rise, for instance, could renovate their homes more frequently.

5 Experimentation: After assessing the demand curves *vis-a-vis* the business insights, it is time for putting the interpretations to the test. Therefore, an experimental setting needs to be planned. To define the experimental setting, three key questions need to be answered. Following are those questions and the reasoning behind these: How will the retailer calculate the profit increase

in the normal course of business? To assess the success of the pricing system, a retailer needs to first set a benchmark against which it will be measured. The retailer may select from alternatives such as control store and synthetic control. A control store (usually a physical store) is chosen from amongst the chain of stores that will continue to use the same pricing strategy as before. A synthetic control is an imaginary made-up store in the absence of a reference or control metric to compare against. It allows the retailer to quantify profit gains. Both e-commerce and brick-and-mortar retailers can benefit from this technique. What is the optimal price change frequency? A retailer needs to choose the frequency of pricing adjustments, such as hourly, daily, weekly, or monthly. This will be determined by two key factors. One is whether the retailer operates as a brick-and-mortar or an e-commerce entity. Two, the accuracy of price change frequency models.

What will be the approach: Exploration or Exploitation? In the exploration technique, a retailer applies new and untested pricing to add vital information to the data regarding the structure of the demand curve. In the exploitation technique, on the other hand, the retailer uses the knowledge they already have from the demand curves to maximise the objective function. Depending on the needs of the store and the accuracy of the historical pricing data, several such techniques can be used.

Once the retailer has answered all of these questions, the retailer will be ready to improve its pricing approach, just like many other retailers. The overall profit will be the objective function to be maximised in most cases, subject to the preferred stock level or sales velocity. The retailer could, however, be willing to increase sales volume or the lifetime worth of a customer. The customer must be involved in the definition of the optimisation issue. Overall, the retailer must present the opportunity report, which highlights several interesting avenues of investigation.

7.4 Marketplace Pricing

Pricing in an e-commerce marketplace is all about being competitive, maximising a retailer's position on the page, and being an attractive proposition in the crowded marketplace.

There are two primary components to pricing and monetising the marketplace platform value proposition. The first component is concerned with the pricing mechanisms – used to price the services or products offered. The second component is the take rate, which is the percentage of the trade value that the marketplace-platform owner will take as compensation for its facilitation, lead generation, and other services.

To guarantee a successful conclusion of a transaction on the marketplace, several tasks must be completed, and the platform owner often assumes part of them in collaboration with the producers. Thus, as an online retailer, they need to familiarise themselves with certain considerations which are as follows:

- Customer Acquisition and Attraction – This refers to the processes that are required to attract customers.
- Discovery/Matchmaking – This refers to the process of facilitating the identification of the niche product being sold by the independent producer and the connection with, the other side of the apple, as they say, the ideal buyer seeking such an experience.
- Trust Building/Risk Reduction – The terms relate to techniques for facilitating transactions by lowering the risk perception and improving trust among the parties, such as insurance.
- Customer Service and Refunds – These refer to dealing with possible post-transaction difficulties that arise as a result of poor quality of service.
- Ancillary Production Services – This refers to any services, such as logistics, that help producers provide the specialised value offer they have created.
- Production – This is the actual implementation of the specialised value proposition core, such as renting a room, providing freelance gig outputs, etc.
- Niche Value Proposition Innovation – These are the methods required to develop the value proposition that independent suppliers give to consumers are referred to as.

The more elements that platform owners take over, instead of providers, the more the platform owner gets entitled to a higher percentage of the transaction's value.

Understanding the best alternative to a negotiated agreement (BATNA) is another important component of sizing a solid take rate. Normally, both parties to a transaction evaluate alternatives before transacting on the platform. The alternative, from the standpoint of suppliers, might be: Demand development and transaction management are self-managed through the use of an alternative marketplace (potentially multi-tenanting, using both at the same time when possible).

If retailers are playing or intending to play in a highly competitive market, there may be a continuous dynamic driving take rates toward a common value. If the market is also subject to winner-take-all competition, the pricing wars – either as a result of an early land grab or as a culmination of focusing on retention – will almost certainly drive take rates to zero. If the market is not yet crowded, the user's BATNA will have to be off-platform, which will make it a little simpler to maintain a greater take rate.

7.4.1 Factors Affecting Marketplace Pricing

Let us now look at the seven variables that influence pricing. See Figure 7.4. These variables or factors are marginal costs, competition, network effects,

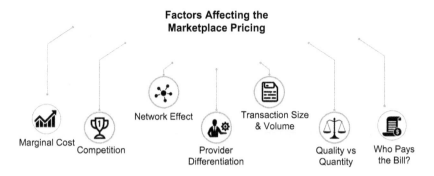

Figure 7.4 Factors Affecting the Marketplace Pricing.

supplier differentiation, transaction size and volume, quality versus quantity, and who pays the bill.

7.4.1.1 Marginal Cost

When it comes to pricing, marginal cost is a crucial factor to consider. Retailers cannot expect to grab a significant piece of their supplier's profit margins if they already have razor-thin profit margins, even if the retailer's marketplace is not involved. For example, on Etsy, the US e-commerce company, the vendor needs to purchase the material, create the product and send it to the customer. Thus, the competition becomes strong because there are so many sellers and profit margins are tight.

Now, consider the stock photo market, which is rather different (as are digital goods markets in general). The retailer may sell a digital product, an endless number of times for no additional cost. Every time a sale is made, the photographer receives 30% of the sale price as pure profit.

If a retailer's marketplace sells a wide range of items with varying marginal costs, they may fix different commission rates for different product categories. For example, eBay and Amazon are two well-known marketplaces that accomplish this. Depending on the product category, Amazon's fees range from 6% to 45%.

7.4.1.2 Competition

Another important factor to examine is the product distribution channel system. Consider whether the retailer is their sole source of information. This might be the case if the retailer can identify a small enough niche that no one else is serving (yet). The retailer will be able to charge more for managing the market if they have a monopoly over a unique product.

An important reason to keep a retailer's concentration restricted, especially in the beginning, is to avoid distractions. For example, when Etsy started, it faced a competitive situation: many of its retailers were already selling on Amazon or eBay. Etsy positioned itself as an appealing alternative for retailers by putting its fees at half of what its competitors were asking. While Etsy loves to argue that it is superior to the competition in many ways, its price approach helped it gain market share from larger competitors, especially in the early days. Etsy has long emphasised that it can only flourish if its sellers succeed. A low take rate successfully expresses this situation.

Although Etsy's costs are now very modest, the site is under a lot of pressure. Since Etsy is a public corporation, its shareholders are demanding more earnings, putting pressure on the company to raise commission rates. However, competitors can still challenge Etsy's position. The competitors may be able to disrupt Etsy by focusing on a narrower market, developing a compelling value proposition for the providers and charging lesser fees.

Taobao's victory against eBay in China is a wonderful illustration of how low marketplace pricing may be leveraged to undermine a market leader. If a retailer is attempting to recruit suppliers from industry leaders like eBay and Etsy to their platform, they will need to either give greater value to their customers and providers or charge lower prices.

7.4.1.3 Network Effect

The network effect is a factor that is strongly connected to the number of distribution channels a marketplace uses. If having more suppliers makes the marketplace more convenient for customers, it benefits from the network effect. This is one of the main reasons why stock photo services have been able to maintain such large commissions. When a stock picture site's collection expands, it becomes more beneficial to customers, especially if each item on the site is unique. Customers will flock to platforms with the largest options because stock photographs are typically needed for highly specialised themes.

As long as a retailer's network is large enough, the bigger the advantage from the network effect, the higher the commission can be. The less benefit the retailer gets from the network, the closer the retailer gets to ideal competition.

7.4.1.4 Provider Differentiation

Most marketplaces in the real world are far from ideal competition. There are many different types of providers. Some are experts who deal with several transactions every day, while others may only sell once or twice a year. This raises an intriguing price question: should all suppliers have the same pricing?

Different marketplaces have used various ways to work around this. People who sell a lot on eBay get special treatment. While the standard cost is not reduced, power sellers get cheaper delivery, unpaid item protection, and promotional incentives. Superhosts receive benefits such as vacation discounts and priority support from Airbnb. These initiatives are designed to encourage users to sell more and retain the platform's most successful suppliers.

7.4.1.5 Transaction Size and Volume

As we have seen before in earlier chapters, psychology plays a significant role in pricing. The fee retailers take from each transaction is the only statistic that matters to the providers. They get suspicious if they believe the fee is too high.

The level of mistrust among providers is not always proportional to the commission percentage. The smaller the transaction's overall value, the lower the anticipated percentage. In general, individuals believe that facilitating a transaction provides a certain amount of value and that facilitating two transactions at $50 each is more useful than facilitating one transaction worth $100. After all, the marketplace provided them with additional jobs in that area.

If the number of transactions by a retailer varies significantly in the marketplace, the retailer should examine if charging the same price for all transactions makes sense.

As a marketplace creator, a retailer needs to develop a long-term business strategy by analysing the market. Such as, how many possible transactions can the retailer expect in a month and what is the overall transaction size. It is recommended to play around with the different factors in a spreadsheet to get the best pricing point for the marketplace.

If a retailer believes the market is large, it is likely to face more competition. This also implies that the retailer needs to keep the prices low. This does not, however, imply a lack of profit.

7.4.1.6 Quality vs Quantity

The key to maintaining high volumes of transactions on a retailer's platform is to provide value to the products offered. The product value is linked to pricing. If a retailer delivers greater product value, and subsequently higher quality, that justifies the high costs.

Insurance for retail marketplaces is an excellent example of how to provide value and improve quality. The supplier and the customer can accept the transaction cost if the marketplace ensures the rented item.

The retailer needs to determine whether to focus on quantity – by obtaining a large number of suppliers to expand their choices – or quality – by carefully curating their selection. In the second situation, the retailer's pricing needs to be higher to express the value it gives. In the former case, the retailer needs to keep the margins low to attract more customers. Both methods might be used in the same marketplace at different times.

7.4.1.7 *Who Pays the Bill?*

As marketplaces have two sides, the customer and the provider – who pays the bill is an essential question. The money is shared between the retailer and the supplier. However, how the retailer conveys this may make a significant impact psychologically.

7.4.2 *Importance of a Marketplace*

Let us look at the importance of running an e-commerce business, especially a marketplace today. The various benefits are depicted in Figure 7.5.

Let us look closely at these benefits:

- Access to More Customers: Visitors to a marketplace are generally more in numbers than those who visit stand-alone websites. Visitors look at these websites even if they are not seeking anything in particular. Though not all visitors are seeking items similar to those offered by a retailer, there is a possibility they will stumble upon the retailer's website. This may result in spontaneous purchases and bring the retailer to the attention of new customers.
- Promotional Deals Management: Customers can get discounts and deals more easily on marketplaces. It also reduces the time it takes to respond. This is advantageous to both the vendor and the purchaser. Sellers may make adjustments to their campaigns more quickly with faster responses.
- Loyalty Reward Programs: When it comes to e-marketplaces, Amazon Prime is one of the most popular reward programmes. It is worth noting that Prime users spend roughly twice as much time online as non-Prime subscribers.

Importance of a Marketplace

Access to More Customers	Finding New Customers	
Promotional Deals Management	Low Extra Costs	
Loyalty Reward Programs	Low Marketing Costs	
Access to Marketing Data	Increased Conversion Rate	
Increased Profits and Marketplaces	Easier Operations	

Figure 7.5 Importance of a Marketplace.

- Access to Marketing Data: This boosts sales to new heights. Marketplaces provide brands with sales data and increased exposure to new customers. Information like click statistics, reviews, and other metrics may help brands enhance their products. Brands can improve their marketing by understanding how potential customers browse for items. Knowing what search phrases people use may help in naming items accordingly. For example, while uploading products, marketplaces like Amazon, eBay, Walmart, and other sites may use this information.
- Increased Profits and Marketplaces: A retailer's ultimate objective is to enhance profit margins. Thus, e-commerce sites play an important role in achieving this.
- Finding New Customers. This exercise becomes less expensive online. A marketplace has a far larger customer base than a single e-commerce site. This effectively implies that by spending the same amount of money on marketing, a retailer can reach a far larger audience. As a result, the cost of gaining a new customer is dramatically reduced.
- Low Extra Costs: The commissions paid by marketplaces may appear to be expensive at first glance. If a retailer wanted to sell products on their website, they would have to pay for a domain, hosting, search engine optimisation (SEO), and advertisements to name a few to bring visitors to their site. When all of these costs are added together, they might easily exceed the commissions charged by marketplaces.
- Low Marketing Costs: It is far less expensive to run a promotion on a marketplace than it is to conduct one by a retailer alone. A retailer can engage in promotional efforts run by the marketplace as a brand. A retailer will not require as many resources to operate this. It also helps to realise that these platforms can reach a larger number of prospective customers than any one business.
- Increased Conversion Rate: Every month, Amazon receives over 900 million views. If only 0.1% of these visitors noticed a particular retailer's brand, they would get about 9 lakh monthly views. Can a retailer get the same amount of traffic? Thus, a marketplace's conversion rate is higher than a standalone website's.
- Easier Operations: Retailers can benefit from the extra services provided by e-commerce platforms, such as Amazon. One such service is Amazon's Fulfilment by Amazon (FBA). Sellers using this service might have Amazon hold their product inventory. The website will then handle the shipment of the items to clients and any other customer support needs. This may incur a cost but it greatly simplifies the retailer's operations.

7.4.3 Marketplace Pricing Strategy

There are many common techniques for e-commerce pricing. However, there is no one-size-fits-all approach. A retailer needs to identify what appeals to the target market and develop a pricing plan that is appropriate for the store. The following are the guidelines to determine a pricing plan or strategy:

Make a Precise Ideal Customer Profile: A hypothetical description of the customer the retailer/company wishes to sell to be known as an ideal customer profile (ICP). The retailer here is describing a customer who is most likely to buy its products, stay loyal, and refer others to them.

1   The retailer needs to identify key qualities of the ideal consumer to create this profile. In most cases, an ICP will include firmographics, which is firmographic segmentation, which is the process of analysing business-to-business (B2B) audiences and grouping them based on their characteristics.

   If done properly, an ICP may aid in defining the issues retailers are trying to address, matching the capabilities of the product or service to the demands of the target market, and helping to set out the future road map for updates and adjustments to product or service. The route to all leads can be through sales, thus it is critical to distinguish between leads who can and cannot buy from retailers since some of them might not be a suitable fit. In this approach, sales representatives won't waste too much time on leads that are unlikely to result in a sale. Retailers may use ICP to specify what constitutes a good match. To get the ideal fit, take into account the following qualities:

   • Budget/Revenue/Company Size: The lowest price point that a consumer would have to pay for a good or service.
   • Industry: Retailers belong to which particular industries or sectors, whether retailers avoid any certain verticals.
   • Geography: Does the retailer sell to a certain area?
   • Legality: Is the prospective consumer base restricted by the law, such as age, geography, or governmental regulations?
   • Limitations on products or services: Does the retailer have a service level agreement (SLA) with clients that commits to a specific response time? Can retailers guarantee that they will be able to satisfy someone's desire for a speedier response?

   This is not a comprehensive list, but it's a wonderful place to start if retailers are attempting to figure out who the ideal customer is. These are the characteristics a leader must possess to purchase from the retailer. Retailer's sales agents will only spend time with prospects that are a good fit if they are disqualified if they don't satisfy all of these predetermined criteria. ICPs don't go too deeply into the people retailers will meet since they are more concerned with how the account fits. Retailers should begin considering whom the sales agents are speaking to and who is ultimately in charge of completing the transaction once retailers have identified clients that suit ICP. Retailers should make sure that the sales representatives are prepared to speak with and respond to the many people they may encounter. These people, who have various positions, degrees of expertise, and product/service knowledge, make up the accounts that suit ICP. Using buyer personas, retailers will further characterise these people.

Moreover, an ICP is not to be confused with a buyer persona, which defines the customer retailers are targeting for the organisation based on factors, such as position, function, seniority, and income. ICPs help retailers match the pricing strategy with current and future customer demands and increase revenue by targeting the correct customers. Everyone in the company, regardless of department or team, should have a common concept of who the ideal customer is.

2 Determine the Desired Characteristics: In terms of both desire and financial means, the retailer's ideal customer needs to be able to purchase the goods. The retailer wants to be a profitable, growing company with a strong network to spread the word about its benefits to other customers. Market data may be used to inform the profile of new e-commerce enterprises, while well-established organisations will already have a customer base of loyal customers.

3 Market Research on Intended Audience: The retailer needs to use information from existing customers with whom they had positive experiences to determine what makes them a good customer and a good fit for the company. Inviting people to discuss why they value a retailer's services is a good idea. Retailers need to communicate they want to improve service and quality and that their feedback is vital. Provide a monetary reward for participating and not ignore any negative feedback and look for similar trends in customer data.

4 Construct a Behavioural Profile: It is time to look for trends in this data. A retailer will want to learn more about high-value customers to attract and retain them. The retailer needs to create a profile of their requirements, reactions and emotional attachment to the brand. It is also a good idea to include their preferences, such as preferred communication methods and social media platforms. By now the retailer may have a comprehensive understanding of the surroundings, pain issues, and expectations of the ideal customer. They should use ICP to evaluate new prospects by running them through a checklist to see if they have any characteristics with satisfied customers.

5 Strong Unique Selling Proposition (USP): It's tough for any e-commerce company to stand out in a crowded industry. But the aim is always to set a retailer apart from the competition in at least one element of the retailer's service and this is a one-of-a-kind selling point (USP). A USP is anything that distinguishes a brand or product from the competition and offers customers a reason to pick the retailer over the competition. It is a means of expressing the retailer's beliefs and demonstrating to customers how the

retailer (and only the retailer) can provide this specific advantage. For example, a retailer might sell handcrafted things, limited-edition items, or just have a larger selection of products than the competitors. Other options include donating the retailer's revenues to a charity or committing to an ethical supply chain. It is easier to settle on a pricing plan when all departments have a clear knowledge of the USP. If the retailer's service is unique and cannot be found anywhere else, the retailer can charge a premium. In most situations, though, the retailer will need to consider competition prices.

6   Examine the Customer Habits: Customer behaviour encompasses both their purchasing patterns and the elements that affect their purchasing decisions. Analysing these behaviours and beliefs will help in aligning the product or service with the customer's expectations. Customer habits are evolving at an increasingly fast rate in the digital age. The desire for faster service is increasing, and from efficient websites to next-day delivery demands are increasing the workload for retail inventory management. Today, customers have embraced internet shopping not just for ease but for reduced pricing. Customers are increasingly expecting a good bargain and are inclined to quit a purchase before checking out if they find the item cheaper elsewhere. However, some habits do not change. For example, setting pricing at $9.99 instead of $10 is still a successful strategy for attracting customers. An appealing e-commerce website is sure to use this.

Similar psychological pricing can be used in several ways in e-commerce. Customers will find it difficult to choose between two comparable T-shirts with identical pricing. However, if one is slightly cheaper than the other, they are more likely to buy the cheaper item since it appears to be a comparatively better deal. Customers can also get a better sense of value by putting luxury items next to lesser choices.

7.5 Impact of E-Commerce

The impact of e-commerce on productivity and inflation will be the most significant in terms of overall economic impact. Through greater competition, cost savings, and changes in seller pricing behaviour, the ongoing spread of internet commerce might put downward pressure on inflation. Since the inception of the internet, the number of electronic companies has exploded.

Each business is unique in its way, with differences in style, promotion, and volume. To be competitive in the internet world, retailers need to keep up with the ever-increasing business transactions. In the long run, a website's net running costs become minimal when compared with the advertising it brings in. Following are some of the changes e-commerce is going to bring in to impact the economy globally:

- B2B Dominance: The global market will be dominated by business-to-business (B2B) e-commerce growth in the next few years. As the bulk of transactions is still done on Electronic Data Interchange (EDI) networks, B2B e-commerce is more complex and greater in scale than direct-to-consumer e-commerce and business-to-consumer (B2C). B2B e-commerce businesses benefit from considerable cost reductions and greater productivity thanks to EDI. In terms of product procurement, transit speed, improved supply chain management, profit margins, and productivity, this has a positive rippling impact on other company activities. As a result, B2B retailers may offer cheaper pricing to customers, increasing their sales income.
- Growth for B2C: B2C e-commerce will have a two-digit growth. Even though B2C e-commerce shop sales are dwarfed by B2B e-commerce store sales and are more susceptible to demand-supply circumstances, the reality remains that it is expanding in double digits. It is worth noting that mail-order houses account for a significant percentage of B2C sales. Pricing methods for B2C e-commerce are highly dynamic and very often. As a result, the pricing of auxiliary items and services is affected.
- Demand and Discounts: E-commerce has propagated an economy based on demand. Customers may now buy what they want when they want, and from wherever they want. E-commerce retailers have also discovered a technique to create flash discounts throughout the holiday season to enhance sales. Customers will be much more interested in shopping online as a result of this. However, when the economic impact of one country or circumstance is perceived in another area, a negative demand pattern is evident.
- Expansion of Sales Platforms: A few years ago, e-commerce retailers began selling through their websites and stores. Customers now have more options due to the addition of mobile applications and mobile-friendly websites to the mix. Messenger applications and chatbots are gaining popularity as new sales channels and e-commerce platforms. For example, customers may shop at Amazon Go convenience stores without having to check out or deal with a cashier. Possibly, more B2C brands may follow suit. This degree of multichannel marketing will increase sales and as a result, have an impact on online pricing.
- Virtual and Augmented Reality: The primary goal of Augmented Reality (AR) and Virtual Reality (VR) is to bring them closer to reality. Imagine if shoppers could see and touch items before purchasing them without having to go to a real store! Customers will be able to have an immersive experience when e-commerce businesses incorporate AR and VR. Customers will be able to see and feel the goods, which will reduce cart abandonment rates significantly. Customised e-commerce platforms using AR and VR will become a reality in the future, shaping the future of e-commerce. There is no question that it will change the economy's pricing dynamics. It will be fascinating to see how prices are managed in the future.

E-commerce is here to stay for good. It will continue to change, as does any business, but for the better of all involved: retailers, customers, and the economy.

7.6 Challenges in E-Commerce Pricing

The following are the current challenges faced by retailers in e-commerce pricing:

- Identifying a Product to Sell: Many hurdles to entering the online market have been removed. Now, anyone can open an internet business in a matter of days and begin selling. For example, Amazon's enormous online product inventory is sweeping the e-commerce industry. Sellers from all around the world can now easily contact customers with their marketplace and fulfilment services. However, this has also made it difficult for merchants to find unique items to sell unless they decide to produce their own.
- Identifying and Attracting the Ideal Consumer: Online customers do not shop in the same manner as they did in the past. They look for items on Amazon (not just Google) and seek suggestions on social media. They use their smartphones to browse product reviews and pay for purchases using different payment options. Consumption patterns and communication online have changed dramatically. Customers are easily distracted by technology and social media. Thus, retailers need to determine where their target customer is and how to effectively attract them – without blowing up their marketing budget.
- Generating Traffic: The avenues for digital marketing are changing. To generate visitors to their online business, retailers can no longer rely on just a single channel. To attract targeted visitors, they need to successfully use SEO, pay-per-click (PPC), email, social media, display advertisements, retargeting, mobile, shopping engines, and marketing affiliates. They need to be visible in areas where their audience is focused.
- Obtaining High-Quality Leads: Online retailers need to spend substantially in increasing traffic to their websites. They need to produce leads to get the most out of their marketing efforts, with conversion rates ranging from 1% to 3%. The funds are on the list. Long-term success hinges on the development of an email subscriber base. It will not only assist a retailer in communicating its message but also enable the retailer to earn from tools like Facebook Custom Audiences. To convert leads into customers, retailers need to develop appropriate messages for each targeted demographic.
- Identifying and Nurturing Prospects: If retailers are not actively engaging with their readers, having a huge email list is useless. Only a tiny fraction of a retailer's email subscribers will become customers. Nonetheless, when it comes to email marketing, retailers need to constantly provide value. Online retailers place a lot of emphasis on conveying product offerings and incentives, but customers want more.

- Conversion Rate Optimisation: If retailers want to seal the deal, they will need to drive quality traffic and nurture prospects. To pay for the retailer's marketing initiatives, retailers need to convert those leads at some point, that is, turn email leads and website visitors into customers. Thus, the process of conversion optimisation is continuous.
- Customer Retention: It costs more to acquire new customers than it does to keep the ones retailers already have. Therefore, retailers need to employ strategies to help maximise the value of their customer base and increase customer lifetime value.
- Lowering Operational Costs: Increased sales are required to expand a business but profitability matters most. Given the pricing transparency, there is a constant demand for lower prices. It is important to constantly minimise inventory costs, increase marketing efficiency, lower overheads, lower delivery costs, and reduce order returns.

Chapter 8

Future of Pricing

8.1 Introduction

The retail industry is evolving by leaps and bounds. Digital consumers who have grown up chatting with Amazon's Alexa and interacting with touchscreens make up the new generation. Grocery shopping has evolved into a new experience – from physical stores to supermarkets to online shopping, not to mention home deliveries by local grocery stores as well as online giants. (Figure 8.1).

For the past few decades now, retailers have reaped the benefits of making the supply chain shorter by taking advance of the e-commerce website. Since the products no longer had to go through the channels of retail, there have been savings in both the physical retail infrastructure and also the cost of shipping to the retailer. With the added convenience of shopping from home (lower cost to the customer), customers can buy at a comparably lower price online which has led to a big change in consumption patterns. E-Commerce still remains a fast-growing area within retail.

Looking forward, we can expect to further increase the efficiency of the retailing process as more and more goods get shipped directly from the point of manufacturing to the point of consumption. Taking out another component of the traditional supply chain, warehouses. With the lightning-fast and inexpensive delivery industry making rapid advances, customers are seeing more and more customised offerings that are being catered to their needs directly by the manufacturers.

Furthermore, customers are using devices such as AI-based voice assistants, internet of things (IoT) sensor-enabled shelves and refrigerators that are taking out the effort of even placing an order with the customer.

The future of retailing is changing, while there might always be a need for traditional brick-and-mortar stores, we are going to see big transformations in the process of bringing goods from the point of production to the point of consumption in the future. It will be a wise idea for future-looking retailers to stay abreast with the potential of new technologies and follow the latest trends of retailing from across the globe.

DOI: 10.4324/9781003382140-9

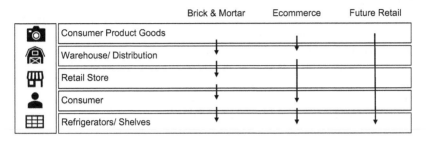

		Brick & Mortar	Ecommerce	Future Retail
	Consumer Product Goods			
	Warehouse/ Distribution			
	Retail Store			
	Consumer			
	Refrigerators/ Shelves			

Figure 8.1 Transformation in Retail Industry.

8.2 Factors Influencing the Future of Pricing

So what is influencing pricing today and what will the future of pricing be? Let us look at some of the factors influencing pricing. These are depicted in Figure 8.2.

8.2.1 Low Brand Loyalty

With multiple choices for purchasing goods and a rapidly changing technology environment, customers are more likely to switch between retailers or even the modes in which they shop based on convenience and price. For example, there are apps now that automatically place orders from multiple vendors to provide a customer with the lowest total price. The app picks the lowest price for each product from different retailers, ignoring any past purchases or loyalty preferences.

Furthermore, online marketplaces behave similarly as they showcase products from multiple vendors and the customer often chooses from one of the options that have the lowest price or the best ratings from other customers.

8.2.2 Digital Currencies

Customers across the world are completely changing the way they pay for their purchases. Very few countries still use cash as a payment method and we are also

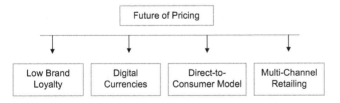

Figure 8.2 Factors Influencing the Future of Pricing.

seeing the slow disappearance of credit and debit cards as a form of payment. With the advent of mobile phones in the hands of all customers, payments are handled digitally using frictionless payments.

Face recognition, smart carts and other security technologies are being leveraged to provide customers with many ways to pay for their purchases while reducing the cost of the overall transactions.

This new form of currency has further enabled retailers and payment platform providers to leverage the data of customer spending to provide customised products and services with customer-level prices and discounts.

8.2.3 Direct-to-Consumer Model

In a direct-to-consumer (D2C) model, manufacturers sell directly to end users. This eliminates a significant amount of overhead cost, allowing manufacturers to enjoy higher sales margins, while still charging consumers less than they would in a traditional retail sale. D2C sales, in some ways, go back to ancient times, when artisans sold their wares to consumers in local markets. The only difference today is that manufacturers can use the internet to transform a local market into a global market.

The shift which began as a retail apocalypse is now threatening other traditional retailers. This is because to challenge e-commerce startups, many brick-and-mortar stores started producing speciality items that consumers could not find online. It was believed that as e-commerce companies were interested in volumes, they were not looking at low-margin markets. This way niche retailers could fill that void and survive.

However, manufacturers of many of these speciality and niche items are beginning to embrace a D2C model. Realising that delivering products directly to consumers can be a profitable business, even if the margins are low. This is now putting new pressure on brick-and-mortar retailers by depriving them of the very business they were thriving on until now. And this new reality is likely to spark a new round of reorganisations, closures, and maybe bankruptcies among the rest.

8.2.4 Multi-Channel Retailing

Multichannel retailing involves selling similar products on multiple platforms through different channels. Platforms can be both online and offline. The various channels are mainly brick-and-mortar stores, online stores and mobile stores. This strategy of businesses aims at reaching out to customers to help them identify a platform for making a purchase that is most convenient to them. The final purchase may occur through any or a combination of these channels.

To survive in today's competitive retail environment, businesses need to make their products and services available conveniently through all popular sales channels. The most effective way to accomplish this is to implement a multichannel retailing strategy. Managing products across multiple sales channels appears to be a strategy best suited for large retailers. Multichannel retail software simplifies the management and sale of products for businesses of all sizes.

8.3 Changing Approaches to Optimisation

Modern consumers are informed and skilled at getting the most value for their money. They have applications that provide discount coupons, they compare prices online as they buy in shops, and they are strongly loyal to the merchants who provide them with the best value. Because of this, your pricing optimisation approach is crucial to a solid and expanding bottom line. Unfortunately, a lot of merchants still base their price decisions on antiquated methods, fads or even their intuition. However, things don't have to be this way. With the introduction of retail CRMs (Customer Relationship Management), ERPs (Enterprise Resource Planning), and pricing analytics software platforms made for businesses, price optimisation has advanced significantly. Businesses may make data-driven decisions and advance their operations thanks to these platforms and the insights they offer. A retail pricing optimisation strategy is therefore crucial for your company. The rapid pace of change that is currently reshaping the retail industry is expected to continue well after the pandemic. Figure 8.3 depicts an overview of this ongoing change. The industry will optimise itself from a data-centric industry to a customer-centric one.

8.3.1 Data-Centric Optimisation

As we learnt, data is the bedrock of every successful pricing strategy. At all times, retailers need to gather accurate product data. The required advertising, marketing, and budgeting are equally important. Whether it is a committed trade expenditure or a discretionary trade spend, businesses need systems in place to record and collect data, display it, and use it strategically.

8.3.2 Product-Centric Optimisation

A retailer that is entirely focused on its goods will always produce newer, more sophisticated items, regardless of consumer desire. The product serves as the foundation for all corporate strategies and operations, which operate as intended.

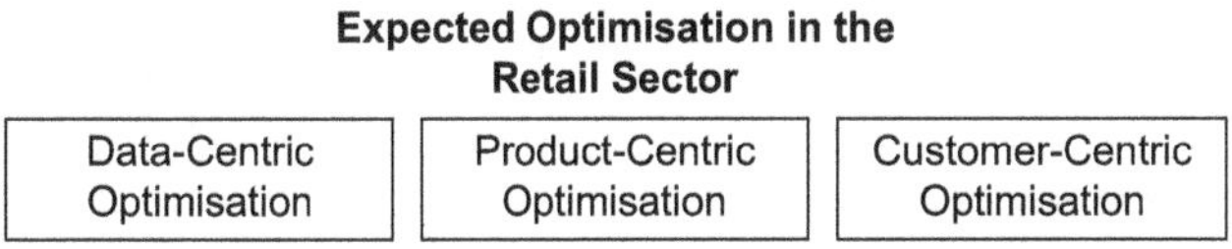

Expected Optimisation in the Retail Sector		
Data-Centric Optimisation	Product-Centric Optimisation	Customer-Centric Optimisation

Figure 8.3 Expected Optimisation in the Retail Sector.

These businesses spend a lot of money on R&D to create cutting-edge items, and they grow by adding new product lines to their portfolio. The business decides to launch any product that is performing extremely well in a market to newer consumer categories or even in a new country. The business decides to make more investments to improve the product quality for the goods that perform better. They keep releasing new, improved versions of the product onto the market. The retailer also decides to discontinue the line of items that are doing poorly in favour of devoting its attention and resources to high-performance products. Product-focused retailers don't operate on the tenet of addressing customers' wants and problems. They operate under the premise that they should provide clients with a product for which they have not yet recognised the necessity.

8.3.3 Customer-Centric Optimisation

Customer-centric optimisation is the next big thing after data and product-centric optimisation. Using granular consumer-level data will help businesses understand their customers. Especially identify the segment that adds to the business's bottom lines, including why they do so, and which products they prefer and why.

Today, consumers have information at their fingertips. They have ample brands to choose from and make decisions only after carefully considering their options, such as the brands available, prices, and product features to name a few. This puts the ball in their court, putting them in a position to be more powerful than before. Retailers need to develop strategies to expand their customer base and retain customers. Having access to granular consumer data and smart analytical tools to turn that data into decision-driving intelligence, businesses can create engaging consumer experiences and personalised offerings with competitive pricing and promotions for their valued customers to stay ahead in the highly competitive market.

8.4 Technology Innovations Changing Retailing

Artificial Intelligence (AI) and other technologies have influenced many industries and will continue to be a big factor in the retail industry in the coming years. As already discussed in many sections of this book, AI plays an important role in many stages of pricing as it is already done today. Some areas where we can see AI being used today include data collection, data processing, modelling algorithms, business intelligence, and competitive data gathering. AI algorithms can be also used to make final pricing decisions that we will discuss in Section 8.5.

8.4.1 Artificial Intelligence in Retail

AI touches up many aspects of retailing today and has impacted operations both in the visible customer shopping experiences and also in the back end by improving the existing operating infrastructure for retail. Below are some examples of AI in action with customer-related experiences today:

- Automated stores with cashier-less checkouts.
- Smart mirrors to help shoppers with clothing decisions.
- Smart recommendations through smart carts, shopping apps or websites.
- Automated customer support and chatbots.

In back-end operations:

- Forecasting and inventory management.
- Assortment management decisions.
- Pricing and promotions optimisations.
- Business intelligence and dashboards.

8.4.2 Internet Of Things (IoT) Devices

IoT devices which have penetrated the retail environment provide several benefits. Not only are these devices helping improve operational efficiency for retail operations, but often the IoT devices can provide a wealth of information that can be put to further use as well. Some examples of how IoT is used in retail stores today are listed below:

- To track the location and delivery status of goods.
- To track the temperature and humidity of produce.
- To reduce theft and loss prevention.
- To enhance customer experience through sensors in shopping carts.
- To maintain even temperature or other storage conditions.
- To track customer path taken inside the retail store.
- To count customer traffic.
- Queue management solutions.

8.4.3 Blockchain Technology

Blockchain technologies can help retailers track products and reliably trace their origins. As the customers get more demanding about the preference of their product characteristics, retailers can leverage blockchain technology to ensure the desired quality of their products is maintained throughout the supply chain, the customers can purchase the products with their desired preferences guaranteed and the right farmers or producers are rewarded for the merchandise being produced. Further, blockchain technologies also enable retailers to avoid counterfeits and prevent supply chain losses. However, blockchain as a technology has been slow to be adopted by the larger assortment and is currently limited to certain areas such as organic produce. If fully implemented, blockchain technology can hold the promise of several benefits as listed below:

- Provide a reliable food certification mechanism.
- Reduce food waste through accurate Condition tracking throughout the supply chain.
- Facilitate faster and seamless payments accurately and quickly.
- Reduce theft, fraud, and duplicating of products in the entire supply chain.
- Provide accurate information on the costs at the product store level to help with margin maximisation.

8.4.4 GS1 Barcodes

While barcodes on retail products have served the retail industry well for over 50 years, the barcodes simply do not capture the information that the retailing process demands. We are seeing the improved version of the barcode via the GS1 barcodes which provide multiple players in the retail chain to gain rich information about the products which carry the scannable GS1 barcode. The advantages to the analytical world of retailing with these barcodes would simply be phenomenal. Many retailers have already adopted these barcodes and an effort is being made to make these barcodes universal.

Some of the benefits of the GS1 barcode are listed below:

- Customers could find out the ingredients of a product or recipe for a dish.
- A customs officer can quickly determine if the product has passed through the right channels and paid the right taxes.
- A retailer can ensure that the product is an original and not a counterfeit.
- Retailers can track the expiration dates at a product level instead of at a batch level.
- Better ability to handle fluctuations in demand throughout the supply chain.

8.5 Technology Innovations Changing Customer Behaviuor

Customers have a wide variety of technology specially made available through personal devices that have fostered new behaviour when it comes to purchasing products. While many of these technologies continue to evolve, traditional and well-oiled retail machinery often plays a catch-up role in the much faster adoption of technology by its customers. Let us take a look at some of the prominent technologies we as consumers have come to adopt in recent years and how these continue to influence our shopping behaviour in today's markets.

8.5.1 Mobile Phone

Mobile phones with internet capabilities have reached the far corners of the globe today. While most European and North American countries see a close to full adoption, we have mobile internet adoption growing in leaps and bounds across the developing economies of the world as well. Entrepreneurs across the world are innovating for their local markets to address the needs of the consumers there. While some have gone the route of connecting the consumers to the products through e-commerce stores, other entrepreneurs have found the world market eager to buy their products directly from various easy-to-use channels. Furthermore, mobile phones are providing a wealth of information that is available to be used to provide custom recommendations on the products the customers would love. Social media channels have provided ways to buy with just a few clicks as they browse through their favourite content on their mobile phones. It is important to note in many cases the needs of these customers on their mobile phones today are met by small businesses and local entrepreneurs and not as much by the larger retailers.

8.5.2 Wearable Technology

With the cost of technology dropping down, many customers can afford smart wearable devices such as smartwatches and fitness bands which also provide rich information that can help the customer purchase customised products and services. Customers can also wear fabric that can communicate vital information regarding their health that can be connected to both the food the customer would need and the medication. Wearable devices can detect important information such as blood glucose or stress levels that the customer may voluntarily use to custom his diet, thus automatically filling their refrigerators with the food they would need on their current body conditions.

8.5.3 Smart Homes/Office

More and more of our actions inside our home and office conditions are controlled by smart devices. Customers can speak to their devices about their shopping lists and ordering preferences. Smart devices can also automatically track when re-ordering for a product is required such as a printer ordering cartridges automatically or a garden ordering the right fertiliser based on soil conditions. Retailers may be well placed to understand and become a part of this growing ecosystem so they can address the needs of the smart customer ahead of the competition which will very well be addressed by an entrepreneurial venture in the future.

8.5.4 Virtual Reality/Metaverse

More time is being spent in the virtual world by customers, this is especially true for younger customers in many developed parts of the world. These customers are very comfortable making purchase decisions inside this virtual world for a real-world product. Many adventurous retailers and producers are making a mark in this virtual world by offering a medium for customers by advertising, helping them make the purchase decision and also completing the purchase inside this world.

8.6 Retail Price Automation

The perfect price for every product is a moving target. The ideal price should match the value a consumer is willing to pay for the given product and this depends on factors that change continuously. No customer wants to pay the full price for produce that is not fresh (Figure 8.4).

To make this more complex, the factors which matter the most for one product location are very different from the factors that matter to another product location. While it is humanely impossible for any category or pricing manager to match the price of products to their ever-changing value continuously, the machines have begun to approach the ideal price more feasibly.

There are several reasons why AI is the next frontier in retail pricing:

8.6.1 Availability of Data

Retail data at the granular level is now stored, processed, and utilised more easily than ever before. The technology allows for efficient processes that can securely utilise input data from sources such as IoT devices, mobile data, camera/image recognition, and store traffic and customer data while respecting the local laws for privacy and data regulations.

8.6.2 Intelligent Algorithms

We no longer have to have highly paid mathematicians writing code and algorithms to utilise retail data. Intelligence and learning are available to use as

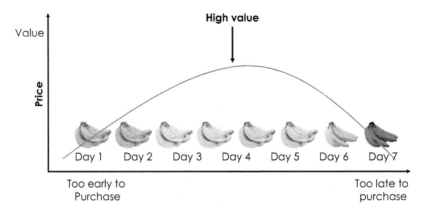

Figure 8.4 Example of Ideal Price Automation for Fresh Produce.

"methods" and "weights" that become the base of an AI-based algorithm to help with pricing in retail.

8.6.3 Instant Output

Retailers now have many installations inside the retail stores such as Electronic Shelf Labels (ESLs), smart displays, employee devices, and beacons that can facilitate the output of algorithms instantly in a store environment. An added advantage is the "feedback" these devices provide back to the algorithms to help decipher if a price is working or if it needs to be improved through "learning".

The technology has been ready for a few years and now we have a solution that can reap the benefit of these new technologies. However, the new system of pricing is not an incremental innovation, it is disruptive. This means the retailer willing to leverage this will need to do so with a futuristic vision to integrate new approaches for the entire pricing organisation. The current situation with rapidly evolving markets will force the adoption in some ahead of others.

Potential benefits of an AI-based Pricing system (Figure 8.5).

The possibilities and the potential benefits of retail pricing are huge with a fully connected AI-based system. While price, promotion, and waste reduction increase revenues, automation reduces costs both at the headquarter and store levels. One of the best use cases for AI pricing is food wastage reduction through dynamic pricing. With a goal of wastage reduction and profit, intelligent algorithms leverage AI to pursue the moving target of the perfect price at any point in time.

8.7 Retail Industry Evolution by Geography

The retail industry has evolved differently in different parts of the world. The evolution of retail has occurred over many generations. While many retailers across the world are discovering the benefits of having a POS system to manage

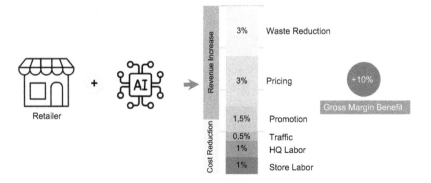

Figure 8.5 Benefits of AI-Based Pricing System.

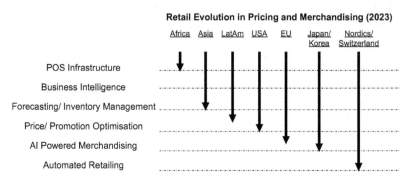

Figure 8.6 Retail Evolution in Pricing and Merchandising (2023).

their cashier's sales transactions, retailers in other parts of the world are leveraging AI and metaverse technologies to have stores that operate without cashiers.

The journey from having a POS infrastructure towards having a fully automated retailing system might be a journey taken one step at a time for many retailers. While at the same time, we might see new entrants in a retail market that leapfrog directly to the stage at which their current market is most suited (Figure 8.6).

In the section below, let us take a deeper look at some of the geographic areas and how the retail industry is placed within them.

8.7.1 Western Europe

The retail industry in Western Europe is undergoing a significant transformation which is presenting new opportunities for merchants. More Western Europeans are prioritising experiences over product lines. so now merchants need to incorporate customer experiences into their value proposition. Restaurants are on the cutting edge of this. Also, consumers are growing more conscious of the impact of their purchases on the environment and communities. Customers want retailers to embrace sustainability, as do their governments.

In 2020, nearly 40% of technical consumer goods sales in 12 West European countries were made online. Click-and-mortar (following the bricks and clicks strategy) retailers were the biggest winners. They increased their online sales by 60%, far outpacing pure online retailers (+36%), and now account for more than half of all online sales for the first time.

8.7.2 United States of America

Today, supply chain globalisation has dramatically reduced the cost of durable, fashionable apparel. The shift away from formal business attire has reduced the number of garments many Americans need to own. Department stores, which rely heavily on apparel sales, have lost their assortment advantage as clothing brands have shifted their focus to direct-to-customer sales, and e-commerce sites have emerged with an almost limitless selection.

Without a doubt, the most significant change in retail this year is the rapid shift to digital commerce. E-commerce accounted for 13% of retail sales in January. In April, that number jumped to nearly 20% of total sales, before levelling off at around 16% by the end of the year. In a typical month, that 3% increase in market share translates to an additional $18 billion in digital sales. The digital trend can also be seen in the amount of traffic that retailers receive on their websites.

The industry has few opportunities to evolve. Yet, every retail brand has shifted from the mall to the mobile phone. The focus of retail itself has shifted from apparel to groceries.

8.7.3 Latin America

In 2019, e-commerce retailers in Latin America produced about 204% more revenue than they did a year ago. Meanwhile, cash and carry merchants saw a 13% increase in sales, followed by drugstores and pharmacies, which saw a 12% increase in sales compared to 2018.

Despite accounting for less than 1% of the retail sector in 2018, retail e-commerce is predicted to rise throughout Latin America and the Caribbean in the next few years. According to Statista, retail e-commerce sales of physical goods will earn over 88 billion dollars by 2024, with electronics and media accounting for the majority of the revenue.

Brazil and Mexico have some of the highest rates of retail e-commerce growth. Brazil is expected to account for about a third of the region's e-commerce market by 2020, followed by Mexico with approximately 29% of the distribution. Meanwhile, MercadoLibre and Falabella are two of Latin America's largest e-commerce retailers. In the fourth quarter of 2019, both companies generated nearly one billion dollars in revenue.

8.7.4 Eastern Europe

Retail has changed a lot in recent years. Nonetheless, compared to more developed markets such as the United States, the United Kingdom, Germany, France, Sweden, and the Netherlands, East European retail is less developed, with more balanced supply and demand (contrasted to more developed economies with an oversupply of retail space, such the US, UK, Germany, France, Sweden, or the Netherlands). According to GfK's (Growth from Knowledge) 2018 European Retail Report, purchasing power in the European Union (EU28) countries increased slightly (+1.9%) in 2017, with Romania experiencing the largest increase (+7.8%). Romania's low per capita purchasing power, on the other hand, reveals a wealth disparity across Europe. There are significant differences between Western and Eastern Europe in terms of retail space per capita.

8.7.5 The Indian Subcontinent

The Indian retail industry has become one of the most dynamic and fast-paced industries with the introduction of new businesses. It accounts for more than 10% of the country's Gross Domestic Product (GDP) and employs approximately 8% of the workforce. India is the world's fifth-largest retail destination.

The 2019 Business-to-Consumer (B2C) E-commerce Index of the United Nations Conference on Trade and Development ranked India 73rd. According to the World Bank's Doing Business 2020 report, India is the world's fifth-largest retail destination, ranking 63.

According to The Economics Times, in India, retail IT companies that provide services such as digital ledgers, inventory management, payment systems, and logistics and fulfilment technologies, are booming. Investors poured US$ 843 million into 200 small- and mid-sized retail technology startups in the first 9 months of 2021, a 260% increase over the same period in 2020.

Due to an increase in online shoppers in India, the online retail sector in the country is expected to reach US$ 350 billion by 2030 – up from an anticipated US$ 55 billion in 2021. Digital wallets (40%) were the most popular online payment option in 2020, followed by credit cards (15%), and debit cards (15%). By 2024, online retail penetration is predicted to reach 10.7%, up from 4.7% in 2019.

8.7.6 Japan and South Korea

In December 2020, retail sales in Japan decreased, while online sales in South Korea fueled an increase. Retail sales in South Korea increased by 5.5% for the full year as a result of the Covid-19 pandemic's influence on the online segment. December retail sales increased by 9%, with internet sales increasing by 27.2%. The main categories driving internet sales were food, home appliances, literature, and toys.

Retail sales generated by local internet retailers climbed 18.4% last year, according to the Ministry of Trade, Industry, and Energy. While brick-and-mortar stores saw a 3.6% dip. The country observed a 51.5% increase in demand for online meal orders.

Growth was also seen in the convenience shop sector, which increased by 2.4%. Meanwhile, department shop sales fell by 9.9% and grocery sales fell by 3% as a result of social distance limitations and lockdowns.

Japan, on the other hand, is still fighting to recover from a 0.3% year-on-year drop in December. The total value of retail sales in Japan for the year was US$ 1.4 trillion, which dropped down by 3.3% from the previous year.

8.7.7 Middle East

The retail sector in the Middle East and North Africa (MENA) has expanded in recent years. A positive macroeconomic environment has benefited retailers, particularly in the Gulf Cooperation Council (GCC) region. Retail segments such as grocery, clothes, electronics, and others have outperformed the world-wide industry average in terms of earnings and returns. With more than 16 billion dollars in consumer spending, Saudi Arabia led the region. Around 2% of the world's top 250 retailers were from the Middle East.

The region has faced various obstacles in recent years, including a drop in oil prices, geopolitical instability, and the rapid advancement of digital technology, all of which have considerably hampered growth in several sectors, including retail. However, according to a survey, more than one-third of customers believe that the retail industry, out of all consumer industries, is set for a digital revolution. Over time, e-commerce has taken a larger share of the retail market. E-commerce is expected to account for 16% of the retail sector by 2025, according to estimates.

Conclusion

The business world is constantly changing and pricing is a battleground. The ability to adjust prices, and strategy in response to changing market conditions is a significant competitive advantage now and in the future. This has already happened in e-commerce and it is starting to have a big impact on brick-and-mortar retailing. To survive in this rapidly changing marketplace, it is imperative that retailers leverage technology and data to devise merchandising strategies based on the best practices that are suitable for their markets.

The future of retail will see a significant increase in online sales and artificial intelligence (AI). The best suppliers will form direct-to-consumer relationships, with retailers no longer acting as the customer's gatekeepers. Intermediaries will emerge to try to control the customer relationship, relegating undifferentiated retailers to a backroom role as a supply chain link. As the industry continues to follow the ever-changing wants and needs of consumers, disruption will affect retailers and consumer packaged goods (CPG) companies alike. Those who can distinguish themselves will continue to thrive and survive. Moreover, the capacity of merchants to provide customers with a tailored, seamless shopping experience will determine their success now and in the future. In order to increase consumer engagement, forward-thinking retailers will focus on developing a route to purchase that satisfies customer needs by fusing together in-store technologies, mobile technologies, cloud options, analytics, and social media into a single platform.

Scientific pricing is trending today. Much of the underlying optimisation strategies, particularly for decision-making by a retailer, has been well established academically. However, the integration of these strategies into a comprehensive system that retail stores can adopt easily is still relatively new. Thus, scientific pricing should be applied at speed to match the pace of market movement and determine the right price at the right time. The insights of all the pricing strategies like competition-based pricing, cost-plus pricing, dynamic pricing, penetration pricing, and price skimming associated with pricing optimisation help retail businesses take their businesses to the required competency levels. Retailers need to undertake real-world field experiments to assess different

DOI: 10.4324/9781003382140-10

pricing strategies and demonstrate the efficacy of price and promotion optimi-sation methodologies. These trials would need to take into account elements like category management, retail competition, unit sales, retail prices, wholesale prices and discounts, complementary and alternative products, promotion activities, and seasonality to maximise category profitability. Different retailers implement the various components of category management in different ways.

As evident, it is difficult to stand apart in practically any section of the retail industry. Spending time crafting brand stories, high-quality products and ser-vices, and memorable campaigns are beneficial. However, there are instances when an intriguing retail campaign is the most effective approach to generate the market buzz that cuts through the clutter. In the short term, a well-executed marketing promotion campaign converts hesitant prospects and raises revenue. In addition to this, if a retailer provides a fantastic product, good service, and compelling follow-ups to new customers, some of them will stick with the brand for the long haul if all the promotional strategies for retailing go well enough.

Markdowns may not be popular in the retail business, but they are required. They are an unavoidable part of doing business. Colours or styles that are unpopular with the customers will only sell if they are marked down signifi-cantly. Of course, when a customer grabs a discount and buys three years' worth of socks, they are taking a significant risk. But temporary markdowns or point-of-sale markdowns are frequently used to encourage sales throughout the store.

Once a store has identified how price fits into an overall business plan, competition-based pricing appears to be a simple technique to adopt. However, especially for larger retailers, given the channels and locations available today, there might be several data points to track who is selling what and for how much.

Correct data at the right time will help retailers make better informed, data-driven decisions in the retail business. They will even acquire detailed infor-mation on customer habits, attitudes, wants, and pain areas with better data, critical for a retail organisation to succeed. Using software-based business intelligence to achieve business goals is a great approach. Solutions that combine business intelligence and data management services with analytics and data integration are what the industry needs to thrive today.

A customer's purchasing choice is influenced by the price of a product or service. Price may be a deal-breaker in the competitive world of e-commerce, where buyers have more options than ever before. Therefore, it is critical to choose the correct pricing plan for a retailer's e-commerce shop. Needless to say, retailers will need to try out a few options before settling on the one or more that works for them. As we saw, there are numerous common techniques. However, there is no such thing as a one-size-fits-all approach to e-commerce pricing. Hence, a retailer must determine what appeals to its target market and develop a price plan that is appropriate for the company.

We even saw that pricing methods are not fixed. These develop and change as new technologies and procedures enable buyers and sellers to form new working partnerships. It is important to note though, today's pricing strategies are not the same as tomorrow's. Pricing needs to be realistic to generate profits. Over the last decade, the world has witnessed amazing technical, scientific, and strategic advancements in all fields, pricing being one of these.

By automating standardised decisions and automating retail, much of the process of retail can one day be left in the hands of machines and algorithms. This future seems to be headed in this inevitable direction, leaving the human brain the opportunity to further innovate to address the changing needs of consumers.

If two people can control a commercial aircraft, there is no reason why a few people cannot control pricing at a large retail organisation.

Index

Note: *Italicized* and **bold** page numbers refer to figures and tables.

2019 Business-to-Consumer (B2C) E-commerce Index of the United Nations Conference on Trade and Development 182

ACOs *see* assisted checkouts (ACOs)
advertising, markdowns with 107
agile pricing 97
AI *see* artificial intelligence (AI)
AI-based predictive business analytics 142
alerting mechanism 121
algorithm developers 24
Altierre Corp. 28
Amazon 1, 159, 160, 163; Amazon Go 150, 167; Amazon Prime 162; Fulfilment by Amazon (FBA) 163
analytics for pricing 55–58, *55*
analytics team 23
anchor pricing 152
anomaly detection 154–155
application developers 24
AR *see* Augmented Reality (AR)
Argos 146
artificial intelligence (AI) 174–175
artificial intelligence-enabled automated pricing algorithms 8
assisted checkouts (ACOs) *see* self-checkouts (SCOs)
assortment analytics 16, 56
assortment-wide plan 68
augmented human intelligence 143
Augmented Reality (AR) 167
automated analytics 143

average purchase price 69

B2B e-commerce 167
B2C e-commerce 167
base pricing 33–72; pricing strategy formulation 33–38; science of 38–51, *39*
basket builders 46
BATNA 158
Beabloo 30
beacons/proximity sensors: benefits of 29–30; companies providing 30; limitations of 30
behavioural pricing 148–149
behavioural profile, construction of 165
BI *see* business intelligence (BI)
blockchain technologies 175–176
brand architecture 49–51
brand awareness, increasing 36
brand hierarchy 49–51
brand loyalty, increasing 36
brand performance analysis 56
brand relationships 48–49, *50*
business intelligence (BI) 17, 23, 121, 129–144, *130, 131*; future trends of 142–144, *142*; mobile 143; perpetual licensing 134; for pricing 139–142, *141*; process 131–132; strategy 129–131; subscription hosting plans 134; techniques 132–134; tools of 136–139, *137*; traditional vs modern 135–136
business/pricing analysts 23–24

CAC *see* customer acquisition cost (CAC)
CAGR *see* compound annual growth rate (CAGR)
cannibalisation effect: markdowns 98; promotions 80
Canon 127
category health monitoring 142
category managers 24–25
category role definition 55–56
category role matrices 58, *59*
cloud vs on-premise 12–14
Coca-Cola 48
Code of Federal Regulations (Section 233.1): markdown regulations 108–109
collaborating vs colluding 127
collusion 127
commodity pricing 148
company strategy 37, 67
competition 159–160; data 53; degree of 115–116; identification of 112–116
competition-based pricing 151
competitive aggressiveness 119
competitive analysis 56
competitive data 11
Competitive Price Indices (CPIs) 38, 125, 141
competitive pricing 112–128; actions and reactions 35; alerting mechanism 121; collaborating vs colluding 127; data availability 122; desired image, establishing 118–119; downward price spiral, avoiding 126–127; examining 35; finding 119–122; market share, gaining 117–118; mechanisms of *124*; objectives 116–125, *117*; positioning, finding 127–128; post-markdown processes and regulations 125–128; real-time monitoring 121; regulations 125–126; setting 122–123; shop mechanisms 120; vendor negotiation 126
competitive promotion 77
competitive reactions 123–125; checking 89
competitive shopping, frequency of 122
competitive strategy 21–22, 37–38
complementary products 46
compliance checking 18–19
compound annual growth rate (CAGR) 27

comp shops 120
consumer packaged goods (CPG) 184
conversion rate 70
cost-based pricing 4, 34
cost per order (CPO) 150
cost-plus pricing 6, 150–151
coupon promotion 76–77
course corrections 66
CPG *see* consumer packaged goods (CPG)
CPIs *see* Competitive Price Indices (CPIs)
CPO *see* cost per order (CPO)
CRM *see* customer relationship management (CRM)
cross elasticity 41–42; formula 42
customer acquisition cost (CAC) 150
customer behaviour: complementary products 46; with markdowns 99–100; market basket 45–46; substitute products 46
customer-centric optimisation 174
customer data 146–148
customer devices 20
customer engagement, increasing 36
customer habits 166
customer level pricing 3–4
customer reactions, checking 89–90
customer relationship management (CRM) 132, 173
customer retention 70
customer shopping behaviour 148–149

D2C *see* direct-to-consumer (D2C) model
data-centric optimisation 173
data engineers 24
data governance 143–144
data hosting 11–15; cloud vs on-premise 12–14; data lakes 12, *12*; ETL processes 14–15
data lakes 12, *12*
data mining 132–133
Data Protection Directive 143
data security 143–144
data visualisation 133
deep learning 150
demand-based pricing 34
demand forecasting modelling 155–156
demographics 10–11
departmental or category sales 69
descriptive analysis 154
desired image, establishing 118–119
diagnostic analysis 154

digital currencies 171–172
digital marketing 79
direct competitors 113–114
direct marketing 79
director of pricing 23
direct-to-consumer (D2C) model 172
discount response modelling 98
Displaydata Ltd. 28
dynamic Pricing 151

Eastern Europe: retail industry evolution 181–182
eBay 159, 160, 163
e-commerce pricing 145–169; challenges in 168–169; considerations 145–150, *146*; customer data 146–148; customer shopping behaviour 148–149; impact of 166–168; marketplace, importance of 162–163, *162*; marketplace pricing 157–166, *159*; omnichannel pricing 146; optimisation of 152–157, *152*; real-time store monitoring 149–150; strategies 150–157, *150*; transparency, maintaining 145–146
EDI *see* Electronic Data Interchange (EDI)
EDLP *see* Everyday Low Price (EDLP)
elasticity analysis *59*
Electronic Data Interchange (EDI) 167
electronic shelf labels (ESL) 123, 179; benefits of 27–28; companies providing 28–29; disadvantages of 28
embedded analytics 143
ending digits 51
End of Life (EOL) 45
enterprise resource planning (ERP) 132, 134, 173
EOL *see* End of Life (EOL)
ERP *see* enterprise resource planning (ERP)
ESL *see* electronic shelf labels (ESL)
ETL (extract, transform, and load) processes 14–15, 19, 133, 139
Etsy 160
Euclid Analytics 30
European competition law 126
European Data Protection Board 144
European Single Market 126
European Union 126

Europe, promotion regulations in 90–94, *91*, **92–94**
events 43
Everyday Low Price (EDLP) 127
experimentation 156–157

Falabella 181
Family Educational Rights and Privacy Act (FERPA) 13
FERPA *see* Family Educational Rights and Privacy Act (FERPA)
5D competitive matrix 115–116
food waste reduction 110
footfall 70
foot traffic 70

GCC *see* Gulf Cooperation Council (GCC)
general advertising 79
General Data Protection Regulation 143
geography, retail industry evolution by 179–183, *180*; Eastern Europe 181–182; Indian subcontinent 182; Japan 182; Latin America 181; Middle East 183; South Korea 182; United States of America 180–181; Western Europe 180
GMROI *see* gross margin return on investment (GMROI)
good-better-best strategy 63
gross margin return on investment (GMROI) 69–70
GS1 barcodes 176
Gulf Cooperation Council (GCC) 183

hardware requirements 25–32, *25*; beacons/proximity sensors 29–30; electronic shelf labels 27–29; inventory sensors 26; IoT devices/sensors 26–27; self-checkouts 31–32; smart cameras 26; smart carts 31; smart digital displays 29; smart refrigerators 26; traffic counters 26
high-level pricing strategy, outlining 34
HIPAA 13
historical sales analysis 55
holiday calendars 53
holidays 43
HRM *see* human resource management (HRM)

human resource management (HRM) 132
human resources 68

ICP *see* ideal customer profile (ICP)
ideal customer profile (ICP) 164–165
image data 53
image drivers 46
image recognition 121
Indian subcontinent: retail industry
    evolution 182
indirect competitors 114
instant output 179, *179*
in-store displays 19–20
intelligent algorithms 178–179
Internet of Things (IoT): devices 10,
    26–27, 175; sensors 26–27
inventory 9–10; control 28; data 53;
    formula *16*; sensors 26; turnover
    of 69
IoT *see* Internet of Things (IoT)

Japan: retail industry evolution 182

key performance indicators (KPIs) 21,
    68–70, 96–97, 137; monitoring
    17–18
Kodak 127
KPIs *see* key performance indicators (KPIs)

last digit/price ending rules 63, 82, 104
Latin America: retail industry
    evolution 181
Levi's 49
line pricing 48, *48*
list price *see* manufacturer's suggested retail
    price (MSRP)
location/zone analytics 56
logistics 9–10
loss-leader pricing 151
low brand loyalty 171
loyalty-based promotion 77

machine intelligence (ML) 150
manufacturer's suggested retail price
    (MSRP) 145
marginal cost 159
margin-based pricing 6
markdowns 95–111; with advertising 107;
    allowance 99; cannibalisation effect
    98; considerations in retail sector
    97; constraints *103*; customer

behaviour with 99–100; data
    infrastructure 100; discount
    response modelling 98; execution
    and weekly revisions 107–108;
    food waste reduction 110; future,
    avoiding 111; identification process
    100–102; negotiation returns
    102–103; networked learning
    models 106–107; optimisation
    103–106; Pareto analysis 100–101,
    101; past markdown analysis 102;
    post-markdown processes and
    regulations 107–111; pricing
    process, leveraging 72; process
    100–107, *100*; regulations
    108–109; results measurement 108;
    salvage value 99, 102–103;
    schedule *108*; science of 97–100;
    sell-by sates 99; space allocation
    100–101; strategy and image
    protection 110; strategy
    formulation 95–97, *96*; types of 97
market-based pricing 3, 34
market basket 45–46
market data sources 10–11
market identification 86
marketplace, importance of 162–163, *162*
marketplace pricing 157–166; bill payment
    162; competition 159–160;
    marginal cost 159; network effect
    160; provider differentiation
    160–161; quality vs quantity 161;
    transaction size and volume 161
Markets and Markets Reports 2021 27
market share 22; gaining 117–118;
    increasing 36
media engagement 11
MercadoLibre 181
metaverse 177–178
Middle East: retail industry evolution 183
ML *see* machine intelligence (ML)
mobile phones 176–177
modelling technique 56–57, *57*
MSRP *see* manufacturer's suggested retail
    price (MSRP)
multi-channel presence, creation of 37
multi-channel retailing 172–173

natural language processing (NLP) 143
negotiation returns 102–103
networked learning models 106–107

network effect 160
new product development (NPD) 25
NLP *see* natural language processing (NLP)
NPD *see* new product development (NPD)

OLAP *see* online analytical processing
   (OLAP)
omnichannel pricing 146
online analytical processing (OLAP)
   133, 139
online behaviour 11
online pricing 120
optimum price 47, *47*
ordering algorithms 16
order quantity 16

pantry loading 81
pay-per-click (PPC) 114
Pepsi 49
perpetual licensing 134
personal selling 79
Philips 127
PlaceIQ 30
planogram (POG) 25
POG *see* planogram (POG)
positioning 37
POS (point of sale) systems 9, 16, 31, 180;
   data 53, 54, 96; monitoring 65
PPC *see* pay-per-click (PPC)
PR *see* public relations (PR)
predictive analysis 154
predictive modelling 133–134
premium Pricing 151
pre optimisation preparation 58–59
pre-pricing 51
prescriptive analysis 154
price changes, monitoring for 66–67;
   competitive 67
price compliance 142
price elasticity 39–41, *40*; formula 40–41
price execution 18, *18*, 64–65
price image/customer perception 20–21
price optimisation 60–64, *61*; constraints
   63; data flow 61; goals 62; good-
   better-best strategy 63; last digit/
   price ending rules 63; pricing
   process, in retail 61, *62*; rules
   62–63; scenario selections 63–64;
   test and control stores 64, *64*
price optimisation plan 60
price promotions 76

price skimming 151
price trackers 65
pricing analyst 23
pricing and merchandising algorithms
   16–17
pricing goals: brand awareness, increasing
   36; brand loyalty, increasing 36;
   customer engagement, increasing
   36; market share or margins,
   increasing 36; multi-channel
   presence, creation of 37;
   positioning 37
pricing manager 23
pricing organisation structure 22–25;
   algorithm developers 24;
   application developers 24;
   business/pricing analysts 23–24;
   category managers 24–25; data
   engineers 24; retail strategy
   consultant 23
pricing process 51–72, *52*; analytics and
   modelling 55–58, *55*; assortment-
   wide plan 68; company strategy,
   evolving 67; data collection 52–53,
   52; data preparation 54; engine *62*;
   framework *see* pricing process
   framework; key performance
   indicators 68–70; leveraging, for
   promotions and markdowns 72;
   measurement and maintenance
   65–67; price execution 64–65;
   price optimisation 60–64; in retail
   61, *62*; roles and responsibilities 68;
   store-wide rollout plan 68; strategy
   formulation 58–60; vendor
   relationships 70–72
pricing process framework 8–20, *8*; analysis
   and algorithms 15–17; data
   collection 9–11; data hosting
   11–15; output processes 17–20
pricing rules 51; selection of 60
pricing solution providers 23
pricing strategy formulation: category
   management 58–59; initial
   considerations 34–35; price
   optimisation plan 60; pricing goals
   36–37; pricing rules, selection of
   60; product relationship
   verification 60; retail pricing
   strategies 33–34; strategic
   components 37–38

private label products 21
private label strategy 38
product-centric optimisation 173–174
product demand 70
product identification 85–86
productive performance indicator 90
product life cycle 44–45
product relationships 47; verification 60
profit/bottom line 20
profit goals of price products 34–35
promotional lift 73, 80, *81*
promotions 18, *18*, 73–94; channels
        79–80; competitive reactions,
        checking 89; considerations 77–79;
        constraints 81–83, *82*; customer
        reactions, checking 89–90; data
        infrastructure 84; execution 88;
        market identification 86; objectives
        73–74; optimisation 87; past
        promotional analysis 56, 87; period
        86–87; post-optimisation processes
        and regulations 89–94; pricing
        process, leveraging 72; process
        83–89, *84*; product identification
        85–86; regulations, in Europe
        90–94, *91*, **92–94**; results
        measurement 89; science-based
        80–83; science of 78; strategy
        formulation 73–80, *74*; test vs
        control process 88; trade
        negotiations 88; types of 76–77
provider differentiation 160–161
public relations (PR) 80
purchase behaviour 11
purchase criteria, understanding 35

RBC *see* resale below cost (RBC)
real-time execution 19–20
real-time monitoring 121
real-time pricing 3
real-time store monitoring 149–150
requests for proposals (RFPs) 71
requests for quotation (RFQs) 71
resale below cost (RBC) 90
retail industry, transformation in *171*
RetailNext 30
retail price automation *178*; data,
        availability of 178; instant output
        179, *179*; intelligent algorithms
        178–179

retail pricing: definition of 1; strategies
        33–34; *see also individual entries*
retail promotions 80–83; cannibalisation
        80; constraints 81–83; modelling
        83; pantry loading 81; trade
        funds 81
retail strategy consultant 23
return on investment (ROI) 28, 75, 131
RFPs *see* requests for proposals (RFPs)
RFQs *see* requests for quotation (RFQs)
ROI *see* return on investment (ROI)
rules-based pricing 3

SaaS *see* software as a service (SaaS)
sales decomposition analysis 65, *66*
sales promotion 79
sales volume assessment 69
salvage value 99, 102–103
science-based pricing 3; promotional lift
        80, *81*; retail promotions 80–83;
        retail promotions, modelling 83
science-based promotions 80–83
scientific pricing 1–2
SCOs *see* self-checkouts (SCOs)
seasonality 42–43, 56
self-checkouts (SCOs): benefits of 31;
        disadvantages of 31–32
self-service BI solutions 142–143
self-service checkouts *see* self-checkouts
        (SCOs)
sell-by dates 99, 106
service level agreement (SLA) 164
SES-imagotag 28
Siemens 127
single customer's profitability,
        determining 35
size relationships 48, *49*
SKU *see* stock-keeping unit (SKU)
SLA *see* service level agreement (SLA)
smart cameras 26
smart carts 31
smart digital displays 29
smart homes/office 177
SMART (Specific, Measurable,
        Achievable, Realistic and Timely)
        Objectives 75
smart refrigerators 26
software as a service (SaaS) 151
SoluM (Samsung) 29
South Korea: retail industry evolution 182

sparse data 57–58
sponsorship 80
spy teams 120
statistical analysis 133
stimulus–response system 149
stock-keeping unit (SKU) 121
store-wide rollout plan 68
strategic pricing framework *20*;
        competitive strategy 21–22; market
        share 22; price image/customer
        perception 20–21; private label
        products 21; profit/bottom line 20;
        vendor relationships 21
subscription hosting plans 134
substitute products 46
SWIRL 30
SWOT analysis 130

Taobao 160
Target 118
technology team 23
test vs control process 88
TFEU *see* Treaty on the Functioning of the
        European Union (TFEU)
T-Log Data 45
Total Response Cost (TRC) 90
trade funds 81
trade negotiations 88
traffic counters 26
traffic drivers 45–46
transaction size and volume 161
TRC *see* Total Response Cost (TRC)
Treaty on the Functioning of the
        European Union (TFEU): Article

101 126; Article 102 126; Article
        107 126; Articles 101–109 126
trend analysis 56
trends 43–44

unique selling proposition (USP) 165–166
United States of America: retail industry
        evolution 180–181
USP *see* unique selling proposition (USP)

value-added tax (VAT) 104
value-based pricing 151
VAT *see* value-added tax (VAT)
vendor negotiation 126
vendor relationship management (VRM)
        70–72
vendor relationships 21
vice president of merchandising 22
Virtual Reality (VR) 167, 177–178
VR *see* Virtual Reality (VR)
VRM *see* vendor relationship
        management (VRM)

Walmart 118, 163
wearable technology 177
weather data 53
web analytics 11
web scraping 120
weekly data monitoring 66
Western Europe: retail industry
        evolution 180
World Bank: Doing Business 2020
        report 182
Wrangler 49